Overflow

Overflow

DONNA SPARKS

BRIDGE LOGOS

Newberry, FL 32669

Bridge-Logos
Newberry, FL 32669

Overflow: Walking in the Power of the Holy Spirit
by Donna Sparks

Printed in the United States of America.

Library of Congress Catalog Card Number: 2022937662

International Standard Book Number: 978-1-61036-275-7

Editing services by Libby Gontarz, libbygontarz.com

Cover/Interior design by Kent Jensen | knail.com

BPI 08/22

DEDICATION

This book is dedicated to my best friend—the Holy Spirit. I would be unable to do any of the wonderful things He has allowed and empowered me to do on my own. Being baptized in the Holy Spirit, with the initial physical evidence of speaking in tongues, and having a close relationship with Him has been one of the greatest joys of my life. If you have not received the baptism in the Holy Spirit, I hope you will begin to seek this precious gift. Jesus desires to pour out the Holy Spirit on everyone who has accepted Him as their personal Savior. You, too, can *overflow* with and walk in the power of the Holy Spirit—only believe!

TABLE OF CONTENTS

ACKNOWLEDGMENTS

Many thanks to Suzi Wooldridge, CEO at BridgeLogos and precious friend, for all the encouragement and for continuing to provide opportunity for publication. Your friendship blesses my life; thank you.

Thanks always to everyone at BridgeLogos for careful attention to every need of my manuscript. Though you remain in the background, your work is essential and much appreciated.

Thank you to my editor, Libby Gontarz, for your wonderful work and for being such a joy to work with. I sincerely appreciate your expertise and quick turnaround.

Thanks to Samantha Carpenter for writing the *Charisma* article highlighting my women's jail ministry and to Chaplain Steven Crino for making the men's prison ministry possible.

And to my wonderful family—how could I ever thank you enough for your endearing patience, love, and for always cheering me on!

INTRODUCTION

I have been blessed beyond measure in my life. I shared my testimony in my first book, *Beauty from Ashes: My Story of Grace*, so I won't share all the details here. But I have been so far from perfect in my life, and it absolutely astounds me that God would even dare use me for anything.

I was raised in an Assemblies of God church and gave my heart to Jesus in that church at the age of nine. But after going through two divorces by the age of twenty-three, I got really mad at God and turned my back on Him. I didn't just turn my back; I completely walked away from Him.

I was a disaster on a road to destruction until that sweet, gentle voice of the Holy Spirit began to draw me back to God. Through the most miraculous intervention, He opened my eyes and completely turned my life upside-down. It didn't happen overnight, but I can tell you that twenty-one years ago, I would have never believed I would be where I am today.

It's not about who I am, because I certainly didn't change by myself. But it's all about who Jesus is and who He has made me into by the work of the Holy Spirit in my life. The thought of continuing on that path of destruction I was on twenty-one years ago sends shivers down my spine. I would never want to go back there. But, my past—no matter how ugly it was—has been the catalyst for making my ministry as effective as it is today. I truly believe that.

I know what the dark side looks like. I know the pain, hopelessness, and inescapable torment of depression. I know what it's like to go to bed at night and wonder if Jesus will return sometime in the night and leave me behind because I've walked away from Him. I know the stubborn pride that keeps us from calling out to God for forgiveness because we feel we have messed up too many times and He's probably mad at us.

I know the fear and paranoia of anxiety and brokenness because of past hurts and betrayals. I know the feeling of wanting to get even and ultimately taking our own revenge. And I know how those actions backfire every single time. I know what it's like to be trapped in a dungeon of unforgiveness and how it can keep us from moving into the future.

I know how self-pity and a victim mentality cause us to be useless and ultimately powerless. I know what it's like to feel no self-worth, to feel empty and estranged from God. I know what it's like to be in the pigpen as a prodigal.

But what's better, I know the way back! I know that we can overcome all these things and more through the power of the cross. I've learned that the Father waits patiently with a robe and a ring, desperately watching for our return, and He runs to us with welcoming, loving arms—not mad at us.[1] I know the process of healing and patiently letting the Holy Spirit do His work in me—no matter how many times I've had to start over.

These are the things I would never want to change. These things have helped me to not only overcome my own problems and weaknesses but also to help others overcome and walk in the freedom and power of the Holy Spirit.

CHAPTER 1

Walking in Freedom

We were never called to be ordinary. None of us were created to be useless or powerless. We can wallow in self-pity for the things that have gone wrong or happened to us in our lives, or we can break free and do what our God has planned for us to do. We can walk in power—His power!

We can dwell on the past day after day, pretending we are the only ones who have ever experienced pain and suffering. Or we can break out of that damp, musky dungeon of self-defeat and make a difference in the lives of others. The choice is ours. We can have as much of God or as little of Him as we desire.

The Holy Spirit is searching for those He can empower, but unfortunately He's having a hard time finding *free* people. We live in a society that embraces a victim mentality. People are always looking for new ways to be offended. Society does not like to hear about sin. They become hostile when they come into contact with Christians who confront their sin. Ever wonder why? Romans 8:7–8 says it best: "The mind governed by the flesh is hostile to God; it does not submit to God's law, nor can it do so. Those who are in the realm of the flesh cannot please God."

We must be totally submitted to God to overcome the flesh. We cannot let the flesh dictate how we live our lives. The flesh craves the things of the world, but the Spirit longs for us to be set apart from the world and useful for God's glory.

"So I say, walk by the Spirit and you will not gratify the desires of the flesh. For the flesh desires what is contrary to the Spirit, and the Spirit what is contrary to the flesh. They are in conflict with each other, so that you are not to do whatever you want" (Galatians 5:16–17).

If we are walking in tandem with the Holy Spirit, we will eventually want to submit to His authority and resist the flesh. As we continually yield to the Holy Spirit, the power of the flesh begins to weaken and our spirit becomes stronger.

Likewise, if we are governed by our flesh, we will walk in the flesh and carry out all the sinful desires of the flesh. The flesh craves sin. Those who feast on sin begin to crave more and more sin. The sin that was once satisfying no longer fills that hunger, so greater sin is desired—leading us farther and farther from God.

You can see this process most clearly in drug and alcohol abuse. When one uses a drug repeatedly, their resistance to the drug starts to increase. Soon it requires more of that drug to achieve the same feeling it once gave them. This process continues until the drug ceases to give the same results unless they use extremely high doses. The decreasing effect often causes the user to experiment with other drugs along with the immediate drug of choice. As resistance grows, an addict will advance to more and more dangerous drugs, seeking a greater high. Unfortunately, that search for satisfaction often leads to an eventual overdose that ends with their death.

We also see the same pattern in sex addicts. One sexual sin leads to another until it doesn't yield the same euphoric effects. This dulling often leads to sexual perversion, sexual abuse, and even sexual crimes resulting in a preposterous misuse of the precious gift God intended for one man and one woman devoted to one another in marriage.

The flesh is greedy, and the enemy of our souls, Satan, is always ready to provide more food for the flesh. He and his minions work day and night to provide more temptations and more ways for the flesh to thrive. He knows that if we feed our flesh, we will starve the Spirit. Sin gives birth to more sin. It's a trap, and Satan knows that sin is like quicksand. Once we fall into sin, we become more stuck with every sinful move. A soul that is consumed with a desire for sin and gratification of the flesh soon becomes an enemy of God. If unbelievers are enemies of God, and we are His children, we should expect that they will also see us as enemies.

Not everyone wants to experience freedom. Many are consumed with the desire for sin and evil. But that doesn't mean that everyone living in sin is unreachable. If we ourselves demonstrate how to walk in freedom by also walking in the power of the Holy Spirit, we will see people set free.

People need to see God moving in power today. They need to know that we serve a God who is alive, all powerful, and completely able to deliver them from any trap the enemy has caught them in. They need to see His power on display, not for the glory of the one operating in it, but for God's glory alone!

They need to know there are genuine Christians out there who *walk the walk*, not just *talk the talk*. Most of those in the world—I'm referring to unbelievers—view Christians as a bunch of weak, boring, and gullible people who are obsessed with an outdated old book of fairy tales. The world needs to see there are true Christians who know the Holy Bible is not a book of fairy tales. They need to know there are those who believe every single word of the Holy Bible, just as it was written, and are not trying to rewrite it or twist its Scriptures to fit an agenda of sin. They need to see people who are willing to surrender all to experience the wonder-working power of the Holy Spirit.

The world needs to see overcomers walking in freedom, godly wisdom, and power. Those without Jesus need to see people who truly believe that Jesus *is* the Son of God and that He died on the cross for our sins and rose again on the third day—victorious over death, sin, and the grave. Because Jesus paid that price for us, we too can walk in victory, walking away from sin, abandoning the victim mentality, and embracing the life of a victor walking in true freedom. The world needs to see us walking in that victory, purity, and freedom.

When we experience freedom, we can experience the true life-changing power of the Holy Spirit working through us. God is looking for warriors, not wimps. We've had too many wimpy Christians running around teaching and preaching seeker-friendly, sugar-coated prosperity messages. We have ruined our own reputations as the world laughs and mocks us for being anything *but* what we were called to be.

They have been amused by the powerlessness of Christians who strut around on huge smoke-filled platforms, fly around on private jets, and live in fancy mansions. They know that the only power these so-called Christians wield is the power of the pocketbook. Many of them have no desire to reach the lost but only to reach the wallet.

Satan laughs at those who preach and teach on the power of God and then walk out of the church and act like sinners. He knows they have no power. He doesn't get upset over those who play church. He doesn't tremble in fear when he sees Christians partying with people consumed with sin to try to "reach them while they act just like them."

The thing that terrifies Satan is when a child of God truly understands the mission they have been assigned to. He shakes in his shoes when he hears a Christian telling people how to escape the clutches of sin and walk in freedom. He burns with hatred when he sees a saint of God walking in the power of the Holy Spirit and doing all the things the Word of God says we can do.

And Satan runs and hides when the people of God get a backbone and get serious about winning souls for God's kingdom. He shudders when he hears a child of God speaking truth when it's not easy or when it's uncomfortable. He panics when individuals share their own stories of how God rescued them, and brought them out of the fire. He knows that when we are set free, we can walk in power—and if we are walking in the true power of the Holy Spirit, signs and wonders will follow. Satan knows he is powerless against a true Holy Ghost-filled man or woman of God who takes God at His word—who believes they can do what God says they can do.

It's time we step up and make the world see that we are not weak, but we walk in freedom through the blood of Jesus Christ! People will desire what we have when they see the freedom we have received, experience the power of the Holy Ghost moving through us with conviction, and feel the tangible presence of God.

I don't know of many true Christians who don't want to walk in power. But we must walk in freedom first. Only when we walk in freedom from sin and the flesh can we walk in the power of the Holy Ghost. We can't be perfect of course. But God recognizes the heart of one who is striving with all their might to truly live for Him and walk in freedom.

Let's get back to work. There's no time to waste. If you need to experience the life-changing power of the Holy Spirit to help you walk in freedom, don't waste another minute. Call out to God right now, and ask Him to save you. Confess Him as Lord and Savior of your life. Turn from your sins, walk away from your old lifestyle, and be made brand-new through the power of Jesus's blood and the work of Calvary.

You are an overcomer!

"And these signs will accompany those who believe: In my name they will drive out demons; they will speak in new tongues; they will pick up snakes with their hands; and when they drink deadly poison, it will not hurt them at all; they will place their hands on sick people, and they will get well" (Mark 16:17–18).

CHAPTER 2

Surrender

"I give myself away." Those were the words I sang from the bottom of my heart when God first called me into ministry thirteen years ago. That sweet but powerful song by William McDowell[2] caused something to rise up within me. I realized that if I truly wanted to be *usable* for God's glory, I would need to give up my own selfish desires and do His will. I would need to surrender my own plans and the desires of my flesh in order to do all God was calling me to do. My heart's greatest desire was and continues to be total surrender to His will rather than my own.

We also sing this powerful song in the jails and prisons. These men and women are beginning to understand the great need to be set apart—to truly repent and completely turn away from anything that might even look like sin. (1 Thessalonians 5:22). They are seeing God move in power. And the idea that God can and wants to use them in powerful ways inspires them.

When inmates come into a church service where the power of God is present and moving, something changes in them. They begin to desire more of God. This is true of not just inmates; almost all who truly experience God's power and a genuine touch of the Holy Spirit will begin to desire more of Him.

The men and women I minister to in jails and prisons are experiencing physical healing, salvation, and the baptism in the Holy Spirit with the evidence of speaking in tongues. Some of them are falling under the power of the Holy Spirit (slain in the Spirit). They know that what they are experiencing is real and genuine. They know it is 100 percent God, and not me. I'm not pushing them down or shoving them to the floor. In fact, many times I'm not even touching them. It's the undeniable power of the Holy Spirit alone. I'm simply a conduit of His power.

We began to see God move in great power among the incarcerated after COVID-19 restrictions were finally lifted. I was beginning to wonder if we would ever be able to go back into the jails. But finally I was allowed back into the Carroll County Jail in April 2021. I will never forget the night revival broke out!

I had been neck-deep in graduation planning, party planning, government issues and meetings, counseling, speech writing, shopping, and more, and I still had to fit in housecleaning before Friday. I was stressed. I was nervous about my baby girl graduating, and I was tired. So when Tuesday evening rolled around and we were experiencing severe weather, I began to consider skipping the jail service.

I mean, the ladies would understand with all I had on my plate. They probably wouldn't even be expecting me in this severe stormy weather. After all, what if the jail lost power? We wouldn't be able to have the service anyway. Not to mention I had a stress headache that just would not relent. It would be a good evening to just go home, rest, and focus on the remainder of my extremely long to-do list.

But I couldn't do it. I know from past experiences that when I really don't feel like going—and especially when the enemy's influences start giving me all kinds of excuses to stay away— something big is going to happen. So I loaded up the projector, my laptop, speaker, and my Bible, and off to the jail I went. It was going to be a sacrifice, but I know God honors our sacrifices.

I signed in and went into the auditorium to set up, and I waited.

And waited.

And waited.

No one was coming. What was going on? I waited at least thirty minutes, but still no one came. Had I driven an hour to get here to find no one to minister to? Finally I pressed the button and asked if any of the ladies were coming to church.

The reply came back, "Yes, we are getting them ready right now."

Finally that familiar buzzer sounded, the door opened, and in they came. It was a bigger group than the previous week, but still not a big group—maybe fifteen. I began by greeting the new ladies, and we started the worship service. The whole time I was praying and asking the Holy Spirit to lead me and give me the words to speak. I had no idea what I was going to speak on, but I knew *He knew* what the ladies needed to hear.

He never fails. I began to preach by the power of the Holy Spirit, and before I knew it, women were weeping. I gave an altar call to accept Christ, and six ladies responded. We prayed, and they repented and asked Jesus to be the Lord of their lives. I often give all the ladies an assignment to read a couple of chapters in the Bible for the next week, and we sing another couple of songs and dismiss. But I always offer to pray with them individually for any needs they have during the ending worship songs.

I had just requested that they read the first two chapters of Acts, and I told them we would discuss the baptism in the Holy Spirit next week. I started the music, and one by one they came to me for prayer. As I began to pray for the first young lady, the Holy Spirit revealed some things about her. As I began to speak the words He gave me, she trembled and wept—tears of joy.

I immediately felt I should ask her if she wanted to be baptized in the Holy Spirit. She said, "Yes! I want everything God has for me!"

I began to pray with her again, and the moment I placed my hand on her forehead, she began to speak in tongues. It was flowing out of her like a river. She was rejoicing and crying and could hardly stand. This lady had given her heart to Christ just moments before. I'm pretty sure she didn't even understand what the baptism in the Holy Spirit was, but she simply wanted more of Jesus.

The next lady came forward and said, "Miss Donna, I want what she got!"

I chuckled to myself, and the Holy Spirit gave me words to speak to her—meant only for her. She began to weep, and before I could even put my hand on her head, she fell under the power of the Holy Spirit. When I helped her up, she was speaking in tongues.

She ran to the back of the room and grabbed a friend and dragged her to the front. She said, "Give it to her too!"

I told her I was not the baptizer in the Holy Spirit, but Jesus was, and if she wanted the gift to reach out her hands to Him to receive it. I prayed for her and gently placed my hand on her head. She immediately began to speak in tongues as the Spirit gave her the utterance. Now, both these women were jumping up and down and praising Jesus.

Then another lady came forward and asked to receive as well. In just moments she was praying in tongues and weeping tears of joy. I cannot even describe to you the presence of God that flooded that jail auditorium. His power and presence was so thick, it seemed physically tangible. One of the ladies said it felt like electricity in the air. Another said she had goosebumps from the moment she walked into the auditorium.

As I began to pray with one of these young ladies, I sensed she was called to be a worship leader. She wept as the Holy Spirit began to reveal His plans for her. She told me, "My dad was a worship leader, and there's nothing in this world I would rather do." She wept uncontrollably and was so excited.

I prayed with other ladies for different needs. A lot of healing, emotionally and physically, took place. I was reminded why I must always press on, *especially* when I don't feel like it.

I sat in the parking lot after that service and cried. I know it had nothing to do with me. The Holy Spirit desires to woo the sinner to Christ. He also wants to empower us to live a life devoted to Jesus and to boldly speak the truth to a lost and dying world. It's not by any strength or ability I possess, but by the wonderful, breathtaking power of the Holy Spirit!

Oh, what a blessing I would have missed if I had chosen to stay home. I certainly didn't leave the jail with a headache. I also had plenty of time to accomplish everything I needed to do the rest of the week, and I did it without stress or worry.

This is what revival looks like. When people realize God's love for them, and they understand their immense need for a Savior, then we begin to experience revival. God desires to pour out His power and presence, but we have to be willing to do things that are uncomfortable.

A few months later we held a water baptism service at the jail. Fifteen ladies were baptized in water. It was the most beautiful thing I had ever seen. Soon after the baptism service, *Charisma Magazine* ran an article on what was happening in the jail. People from all over began to read the story of God's wonder-working power.[3]

I am so blessed to say that revival is still going strong in the jail. A few weeks ago I went in to minister, and the power of the Holy Ghost filled the room so powerfully I was in awe. Every lady present was baptized in the Holy Spirit with the evidence of speaking in tongues!

There was so much weeping and laughter as ladies were filled to overflowing with the Holy Spirit. At the end of the service, each one shared her testimony of being baptized in the Holy Spirit. I shared the short clip on my social media page, and people were amazed and moved to tears as they listened to these ladies.

A couple of days later a friend contacted me to tell me that she shared that short audio clip with her church family, and revival broke out in their church. Many were baptized in the Holy Spirit with the evidence of speaking in tongues in their church service!

God wants to pour out His power and presence in our lives. The Holy Spirit longs to fill us so full that we will overflow onto everyone we come into contact with. When we are powered up, people notice. Not only do they notice, they begin to desire what we have.

But are we willing to completely surrender to see the miraculous happen in our lives?

When we are full of the Holy Spirit and totally surrendered to Him, it truly makes a difference. Smith Wigglesworth was a great healing evangelist of the late 1800s to early 1900s. He attributed the success of his ministry to his personal relationship with the Holy Spirit. Smith once told the story of spending a season of praying in the Holy Ghost before he went on a trip. He had spent so much time praying in the Spirit that when he boarded the train, people around him began to say, "I'm convicted of my sins because of you!" They began to weep or to get up and move away from him. He never had to speak a word. The power of the Holy Spirit emanated from him so powerfully that people felt convicted of sin, and began to repent or had to leave.[4]

Can you imagine what it would be like if we walked in that kind of power? If enough of us carried that kind of anointing, we could change the world. I don't know about you, but I desire that kind of power and anointing more than anything else in this world.

I tell everyone that the Holy Spirit is my best friend. And I mean it with all my heart. I could do nothing without Him. I was a total introvert until He filled me and empowered me to preach the gospel. I love Him and I don't want to grieve Him. I know that He can do more in a person's life than I could ever teach. That is why I desire to see others filled with the Holy Spirit.

I know from experience what His power has accomplished in my life. If He did it for me, He can certainly empower others to do these things and even more.

The Christian life does not have to be boring or mundane. We can live a life of power and victory if we will completely surrender to God's will. The Christian who tries to live their life halfway in and halfway out will be the most miserable person alive.

There is no joy in halfway doing anything. That's why Jesus said He would rather we would be cold or hot. "I know your deeds, that you are neither cold nor hot. I wish you were either one or the other! So, because you are lukewarm—neither hot nor cold—I am about to spit you out of my mouth" (Revelation 3:15–16).

Oh how I wish I could get hold of the fire and zeal of some of the old-time evangelists. I'm always inspired to learn of how God used them in such powerful ways. That's why I am determined to press on. I won't give up until He uses me in the same kind of ways.

If He did it for them, He can do it for us. God is no respecter of persons (Acts 10:34). And God is the same yesterday, today, and forever. If He used others for great purposes, He will use us also. Since He does not change, we can believe He will do the miraculous just as He did in the time of the New Testament.

If we are not walking in power, we only have ourselves to blame. What do we need to surrender?

CHAPTER 3

The Baptism in the Holy Spirit

Confusion often surrounds the person of the Holy Spirit—the third person of the Trinity—and the power of the Holy Spirit. There's even more confusion in many circles when we talk about the baptism in the Holy Spirit. What does it all mean?

Many people have quit speaking of the Holy Spirit and His power entirely; I believe this is because they feel they don't really understand Him at all. But as I said, the Holy Spirit is just as much a person as—and coequal with—Jesus and God the Father. He is the third person of the Trinity.

However, because there are so many facets to the Holy Spirit, we can sometimes become confused. That's why in this chapter, I want to discuss the baptism in the Holy Spirit, which is accompanied by speaking in tongues as the evidence. One of the questions I'm asked most often is, *If I receive the Holy Spirit when I repent and get saved, why do I need to receive the* baptism in *the Holy Spirit?* Good question.

When we surrender our hearts to Christ, ask Him to forgive us of our sins, and choose to make Him the Lord of our lives, we receive what I call a deposit of the Holy Spirit. Our rebirth itself is the activity of the Holy Spirit. The Holy Spirit initially indwells us at the time of salvation to convict us of sin and to lead us into sanctification and holiness. He also helps us to understand the Scriptures in the Holy Bible more clearly.

When Jesus breathed on His disciples and told them to receive the Holy Spirit (John 20:22), they were immediately born again of the Spirit and received power to bring glory to God. But the Comforter had not yet come, so Jesus sent them to the upper room to wait for the gift the Father had promised—the *baptism* in the Holy Spirit (Acts 1:4–5). When we are baptized in the Holy Spirit subsequent to salvation, it's like we are baptized or drenched from the inside out. We become so full of the Holy Spirit on the inside, He just begins to overflow right out of us. That overflow is accompanied with an unknown language that spills out of our mouths.

I struggled to receive the Holy Spirit for many years because I believed God would just take control of my mouth and tongue and cause words to start coming out uncontrollably. And that didn't happen.

We must realize that just as we receive our salvation through faith in Christ's finished work on the cross, and in His death and resurrection, we also receive the Holy Spirit by faith in what the Father has promised us. "I am going to send you what my Father has promised; but stay in the city until you have been clothed with power from on high" (Luke 24:49).

On one occasion, while he was eating with them, he gave them this command: "Do not leave Jerusalem, but wait for the gift my Father promised, which you have heard me speak about. . . . But you will receive power when the Holy Spirit comes upon you" (Acts 1:4, 8).

The Holy Spirit is gentle. He will never make you do anything you don't want to do. So you don't have to worry about acting crazy or doing something that would embarrass you. And, you must ask God for the gift of the Holy Spirit to receive it. God is not going to give you something you don't desire.

If you know Jesus as your Savior and you are following Him with all your heart, you only need ask Him to give you the gift of the Holy Spirit and He will fill you.

Ask and it will be given to you; seek and you will find; knock and the door will be opened to you. For everyone who asks receives; the one who seeks finds; and to the one who knocks, the door will be opened. Which of you, if your son asks for bread, will give him a stone? Or if he asks for a fish, will give him a snake? If you, then, though you are evil, know how to give good gifts to your children, how much more will your Father in heaven give good gifts to those who ask him! (Matthew 7:7–11)

In the jail and prison church services, I have seen men and women repent of their sins, ask Jesus to become their Savior, and only minutes later receive the baptism in the Holy Spirit and begin to speak in tongues. I have seen other people who have served Jesus faithfully for years and have asked to receive the Holy Spirit and still haven't received the gift. Does that mean that some people just can't receive the Holy Spirit? No. God is not a respecter of persons. He wants all to receive this wonderful gift. But we must surrender and be willing to speak out in faith the utterances He gives us.

Many people have told me, "I'm afraid to say what comes to mind because I'm afraid I'm making it up."

And I reply, "That is exactly what Satan wants you to believe. If he can convince you not to speak it out in faith, he can hinder you from receiving the gift. And he wants nothing more than to keep you from the power the Holy Spirit will bring to your life!"

Remember, it's a step of faith. We must open our mouths and prepare to speak what God puts in there! The very minute you speak it out, it will begin to flow from your innermost being, and you will know you have received the baptism in the Holy Spirit. Therefore, tongues are a sign of the baptism in the Holy Spirit.

But, why do we want to receive the gift of the Holy Spirit? I'm going to share with you some of the reasons I have found the baptism in the Holy Spirit to be so very important in my own life.

HE GUIDES US IN ALL TRUTH

"I have much more to say to you, more than you can now bear. But when he, the Spirit of truth, comes, he will guide you into all the truth. He will not speak on his own; he will speak only what he hears, and he will tell you what is yet to come" (John 16:12–13).

When I was called into ministry I was elated. I wanted to know exactly what I would be doing for God. What would my ministry look like? When would it happen? How would it happen?

However, at that point in my life, the Holy Spirit only revealed to me the fact that I had a calling on my life. He didn't share a lot of details about what it would look like or how I would get there. I wanted to see the big picture at the very beginning, but that wasn't happening. Looking back now, I realize it was best that I didn't know all the details.

I'm sure I would have tried to make things happen in my own way and my own timing, and I would have gotten in God's way. Just as Jesus told the disciples, "I still have many things to say to you, but you cannot bear them now" (John 16:12 ESV), I didn't need to know everything in the beginning.

There's still so much I'd love to know about how my ministry will look in the days ahead, but I have learned the value of allowing the Holy Spirit to lead me in God's perfect timing. I know that He will guide me in the *truth* of what God has in store for me instead of allowing me to jump to conclusions about what I *think* I should be doing.

The Holy Spirit has also protected me from the opinions of others who think they know what God has called me to do. We often have very well-meaning people in our lives who want to give us a "word" about what God is calling us to do.

I've had people close to me who have told me I was called to do one thing or another, and at the time those things sounded like grand ideas. Without having the Holy Spirit to guide me in all truth, I could have pursued something that was more of a distraction than a calling.

It wasn't that they were bad things, and the people who told me those things meant no harm. It was just that those things were not the perfect will of God. They would have taken me off course from what God was truly directing me into, prolonging my journey. His will would still have been accomplished, but I might have had more struggles in getting there.

The Holy Spirit is the perfect navigator. He helps us to stay on track because He leads us in and helps us to discern the truth.

THE HOLY SPIRIT TELLS US WHAT IS TO COME

Just as we read in John 16:13, the Holy Spirit tells us of things to come. I have experienced this in many ways in my life. Sometimes the Holy Spirit will share with us in detail what is to come, and at other times He will simply prepare us for what is ahead.

While speaking in churches, I have often shared about an incident when I was on the way to minister in jail, and the Holy Spirit came upon me in such power, I could do nothing but pray in tongues all the way to the facility!

When I began the worship service, a demon began to manifest in one of the inmates. I was not expecting that to happen! In fact, I had never experienced that happening in a jail service before. But I had perfect peace, and with the guidance of the Holy Spirit, I was able to cast out the demon and continue the service peacefully.

I know without a doubt the Holy Spirit was preparing me on the way to the jail for what I was going to encounter while there. Even though I didn't know what was coming, He knew exactly what was to come, and He was strengthening me in faith and in power.

As we watch the news today and see the troubling things in our world, I believe the Holy Spirit shows us and reveals to us that Jesus is coming soon. We don't have to fear the future when we see these things. When the Holy Spirit reveals the things that are to come, He also gives us a sense of peace about it if we are striving to live our lives for Jesus.

PRAYING IN TONGUES
MAKES YOU STRONG

Now, let's go even deeper into why we need to pray in tongues when we have been baptized in the Holy Spirit.

Just as I spoke of how the Holy Spirit prepared me to cast out demons before I got to the jail, He has also empowered me in other areas of my life with a boldness that I could not have experienced without His power.

"Anyone who speaks in a tongue edifies themselves" (1 Corinthians 14:4). When we speak of *edifying* ourselves, it means to make ourselves strong. If we want to make our muscles stronger, we go to the gym and lift weights. If we want to become stronger in our spiritual lives, we pray in tongues.

The Holy Spirit edifies us, and causes us to be stronger in faith so that we can carry out the works of God.

I never step onto a platform to preach without spending many hours praying in tongues. I know I have no power of my own, but I know the Holy Spirit is strong within me. He will give me the power and boldness to say the things that I would normally be uncomfortable saying.

In these last of the last days, we need the strength and power to speak the things that are hard to say in the world we live in. We can only do that with the boldness and power of the Holy Spirit. We need Him to come help build us up and increase our faith. "But you, dear friends, by building yourselves up in your most holy faith and praying in the Holy Spirit, keep yourselves in God's love as you wait for the mercy of our Lord Jesus Christ to bring you to eternal life" (Jude 20–21).

PRAYING IN TONGUES
HELPS CLEAN UP YOUR MOUTH

When a sinner comes to Jesus, they still have old habits that linger and are hard to surrender. James tells us that the tongue is unruly and hard to tame. "Those who consider themselves religious and yet do not keep a tight rein on their tongues deceive themselves, and their religion is worthless. . . . but no human being can tame the tongue. It is a restless evil, full of deadly poison" (James 1:26; 3:8).

Oh how hard it is to tame the tongue, but we can do it with the Holy Spirit's help. During one of our most powerful services in the jail, every lady present was baptized in the Holy Spirit with the evidence of speaking in tongues. The transformation that began to take place in their lives was beyond anything I had seen.

These ladies had repented and had been living for Jesus for quite some time, but many of them still had trouble controlling their tongues because of bad habits. Some of them had pretty filthy mouths!

One night one of my sweet ladies came into the service and said, "Mrs. Donna, I have to tell you something. I used to be a real potty mouth! But now if I cuss, I feel so bad I have to repent immediately. I can't stand those words anymore."

Another lady spoke up and said, "I know exactly what you mean. If I even hear someone say a curse word, it feels like someone is stabbing me with a knife! I used to listen to rap music with all kinds of filthy language, and it never bothered me. I'll never be able to listen to it again!"

No matter how many times I told them to clean up their talk, it didn't matter to them. But after being filled with the Holy

Spirit, He has helped them clean it up. We don't want to grieve the Holy Spirit, and when we begin to use foul language or gossip about others, that is exactly what we are doing.

He gently convicts us and pulls us back into alignment with God's will for us. If we will choose to listen to Him and be obedient, He will most definitely clean up a potty mouth!

PRAYING IN TONGUES REFRESHES US

I don't know about you, but there are a lot of times when I just feel spiritually worn out. Sometimes I feel like I have given and given and given everything that is within me, and I just need to be filled back up.

I can sit down and spend some time praying in tongues, and before long I feel recharged and refreshed. There's not a vitamin or energy drink on this planet that can do for me what the power of the Holy Spirit can do in me with just a few minutes of praying in tongues. We must pray to be refilled continually, if we want to experience this refreshing.

The disciples also prayed to be refilled and were refreshed after they initially received the baptism in the Holy Spirit. After Peter and John were arrested for healing the lame man in the name of Jesus, they went back to their own people once they were released. After telling them what they had experienced with the chief priests and elders, they prayed together and experienced a refreshing! "After they prayed, the place where they were meeting was shaken. And they were all filled with the Holy Spirit and spoke the word of God boldly" (Acts 4:31).

If they needed a refreshing, we can certainly benefit from being revived and refreshed as well.

PRAYING IN TONGUES
GIVES US POWER TO WITNESS

I believe the main reason for the baptism in the Holy Spirit is to give us the power to witness to others. Jesus Himself told the disciples to wait until they were clothed with power from on high before they attempted to go and spread the Gospel.

We can see the immediate effect on Peter after he was baptized in the Holy Spirit. After the disciples were assumed to be drunk because they were speaking in tongues, this happened:

> Then Peter stood up with the Eleven, raised his voice and addressed the crowd: "Fellow Jews and all of you who live in Jerusalem, let me explain this to you; listen carefully to what I say. These people are not drunk, as you suppose. It's only nine in the morning! No, this is what was spoken by the prophet Joel:
>
> "In the last days, God says,
>   I will pour out my Spirit on all people.
> Your sons and daughters will prophesy,
>   your young men will see visions,
>   your old men will dream dreams.
> Even on my servants, both men and women,
>   I will pour out my Spirit in those days,
>   and they will prophesy." (Acts 2:14–18)

Peter had denied Christ three times in his own strength. But after being baptized in the Holy Spirit, he experienced a new boldness and authority that equipped him with the power to boldly testify and share the Gospel. Three thousand were converted to Christianity that day as a result of the power that was demonstrated through Peter's testimony.

I have spoken many times of how I was a total introvert before I was baptized in the Holy Spirit. I didn't like crowds. I didn't talk to people if I didn't have to. And I can promise you, I would have never volunteered to stand before a group of people and speak.

The power of the Holy Spirit in my life has brought me out of that shell. I now gladly and boldly proclaim the testimony of Jesus Christ, and I jump at every opportunity to share the gospel with anyone. I know this is not because of any power I possess, but only by the mighty power of the Holy Spirit within me.

I am so very grateful for everything the Holy Spirit does, and how He helps me in every area of my life. You can probably understand now why I refer to Him as my best friend.

CHAPTER 4

The Holy Spirit's Transforming Power

I could talk about the Holy Spirit all day long and tell you about all the wonderful ways He has worked in my life. I know what I would be without Him—weak and powerless at the very least. I dare not take a single step without Him. His is the power that makes my ministry effective. I have no power of my own, but as I have learned to surrender my will to His, I have seen Him transform the lives of so many.

I could never accomplish in one hundred years what He is able to do in just minutes. His is the power of transformation through conviction, with a tender loving voice that draws us ever so gently, but oh so powerfully, to the foot of the cross. I simply adore Him.

I could try to put into words some of the many transformations I have seen Him perform right before my eyes, but I decided to let some of my dearest friends share their stories with you. I speak often of my "jail ladies." These are the ladies I minister to on a regular basis in jails and prisons.

I asked them to write their own stories to share with you the amazing life-changing power of the Holy Spirit that they have experienced in their own lives. These are their stories in their own words.

My name is Barbara Austin, and I am only here by God's grace. The enemy and his influences began trying to destroy my life at the age of five years old when my uncle was murdered right in front of me by a gunshot blast to the head. Soon afterwards, my mother and another of my uncles were sent to prison.

For the next ten years of my life I was repeatedly raped and molested. Finally at the age of fifteen, I mustered up the courage to fight back, and it stopped. Unfortunately by the age of eighteen, while on vacation, a man subdued me and began raping me, and I defended myself.

Because of this, I received a second degree murder charge, making me a convicted felon at the age of eighteen. At this point I began partying and using drugs to numb the pain. I have also battled with homosexuality from the age of seven years old.

When I thought things couldn't get worse, my grandmother—a devout prayer warrior, my strength, and my best friend—passed away.

I became suicidal after that, feeling no reason to continue living in such pain and agony. But once again it got worse when one year later I received a phone call to inform me my mother had been murdered. Not to mention, all of my family had turned their backs on me at this point. Deep dark depression set in, and eventually I had a mental breakdown.

After a repeated mental breakdown five months after the first, I decided to commit suicide. But by the grace of God, the gun that was pointed at my head did not go off. When I removed it, the gun fired at the ground. Not knowing what else to do, I called the police, and they arrested me.

I served fifteen months in the Cumberland County Jail before being sent to the Carroll County Jail to work. Since I have been here, I have repented of my sins and asked Jesus to be my Savior. I have truly grown closer to God, and one of my greatest joys was becoming baptized in the Holy Spirit with the evidence of speaking in tongues.

I'm so blessed to know that I have a prayer language through the Holy Spirit that can not be deciphered by the enemy of my soul—Satan. I know the Spirit prays on my behalf when I don't know what I should pray for myself.

> In the same way, the Spirit helps us in our weakness. We do not know what we ought to pray for, but the Spirit himself intercedes for us through wordless groans. And he who searches our hearts knows the mind of the Spirit, because the Spirit intercedes for God's people in accordance with the will of God. (Romans 8:26–27)

Since I have been baptized in the Holy Spirit, I have been more at peace, and have had increasing joy in my life. Though it may seem small, I now have the faith of a mustard seed, and I truly believe I can move mountains by faith. "Truly I tell you, if you have faith as small as a mustard seed, you can say to this mountain, 'Move from here to there,' and it will move. Nothing will be impossible for you" (Matthew 17:20).

I am so very grateful for God's mercy and grace in my life. I truly hope my testimony can help someone else out there who may be going through the same things I have been through. If we truly seek God in all we do, He will be right by our side, even when we may not feel like He is.

And when we are baptized in the Holy Spirit with the evidence of speaking in tongues, we truly will become stronger and better equipped to overcome the sin the enemy so desperately tries to destroy our lives with. The Holy Spirit makes us bold in our faith, and helps us to overcome temptation.

I am so very proud of Barbara. The change I have seen in her life is undeniable. I believe God is going to use Barbara in powerful ways to help rescue others from the grips of sin. The Holy Spirit's transformation is so beautiful in our lives. There is no one so far from Him that they can't be reached by the love and grace of God. I love how He cares for us and pursues us, just like He has pursued Barbara.

Next is Traci's story.

My name is Traci, and I'm fifty-four years old. I have been in active addiction for several years off and on. But, by the grace of God, I have been redeemed and recovered, and I don't plan on going back to my former way of life.

There's really no better feeling than being clean and being in a right relationship with Christ. I'm very thankful to have come from a good, loving family, and now they are so proud of me because they have seen the change in me. I once was lost, but now I'm totally on fire for God.

I am so glad I now have Him in my life; without Him I don't know where I would be. I know deep down His purpose was to send me to this jail for a while. I always believed in Jesus, but after rededicating my life to Him, and drawing closer to His side, I began to desire more of Him. Because of my hunger for more of Him, I was finally baptized in the Holy Spirit with the evidence of speaking in tongues. There is absolutely nothing like the peace and joy down in your soul, and the great love in your heart you feel from Him.

There are still things I'm working on, but I know that the Holy Spirit is working through them with me. He is leading me, correcting me, and teaching me, and I am overcoming with Him by my side! I feel like He truly is my best friend. I wish everyone could experience this wonderful gift that I've been given.

And you can! You need only to believe, and ask to receive. I hope this verse will speak to you. "May the God of hope fill you with all joy and peace as you trust in him, so that you may overflow with hope by the power of the Holy Spirit" (Romans 15:13).

Traci is another precious lady I am so very proud of. I cannot begin to tell you how I have seen her blossom since she was baptized in the Holy Spirit. It's almost as if she glows when she walks into the room. She always has a smile on her face, and she worships God with her whole heart.

I sense a deep peace in her that wasn't there before, and I know God is going to use her in tremendous ways.

I will share one more story with you before I conclude this chapter.

My name is Tracy Wallace, and I have been a drug addict and alcoholic for twenty-five years. I have spent more than half my life in jails and prisons, but by the grace and mercy of God, I have been cleansed and made new from the inside out.

As a child, I was taken to church by my aunt up until the age of twelve.

When I was twelve, my grandparents, whom I lived with up until that point, died. My mother finally stepped in and took responsibility for me.

I have two children, and unfortunately my son followed in my footsteps as he is also serving time in prison. I have been in many mentally as well as physically abusive relationships off and on throughout my life until I met my beloved fiancé in 2015.

My world came crumbling down around me in 2019 when my fiancé died. I completely gave up on life, but my biggest mistake was giving up on God. I was completely done with Him, but He wasn't done with me.

After six months of gradually relapsing—after one year of sobriety—I fell headlong back into my addiction and destructive lifestyle. I finally realized there was only one way out of this dark pit I had dived back into. I knew I had to call out to God.

Right then and there, I began to call out to God, "Save me, save me, save me!" Three and a half hours later, I was at a friend's house. No one knew I was there, but miraculously, the police came and arrested me. That was definitely God!

I decided upon arriving at the jail that I was going to finally rededicate my life to the Lord and follow His will for my life. For two years, I have plunged myself into the reading of His Holy Word, the Bible, and spending time in prayer. I have been seeking His guidance and direction for my life.

I am living proof that there is hope and a future with Jesus Christ our Lord! Praise God! I have repented of my sins, and was baptized in the Holy Spirit with the evidence of speaking in tongues. I have been physically healed from nerve pain in my back and hip that almost prevented me from being able to walk.

He has restored a relationship between me and my daughter and grandkids after twenty-eight years apart. The Holy Spirit has truly changed me from the inside out. I have received so much healing both mentally and emotionally. The Holy Spirit has truly changed my entire life for the better. He leads and guides me, corrects me when I sin, and has changed the way I see, feel, and think about things.

I have learned when times get tough, it's an opportunity to learn to hold onto Him and His Word. I know it is all about seeking Him and what He is trying to show me so I can grow in the knowledge of Him.

It's so easy to fall into the enemy's trap, but we must remember that his ways lead only to death and destruction. But God's desire is to lead us to life and life more abundantly through Him! "The thief does not come except to steal, and to kill, and to destroy. I have come that they may have life, and that they may have it more abundantly" (John 10:10 NKJV).

I'm now pursuing a life of sharing the gospel with others who need hope, love, and forgiveness. God has placed a burning desire in my heart to go out and reach the lost with His good news. I hope I can inspire others to also go out and share the gospel, to seek God and all He has for you, and to be a blessing to others.

The only way to a truly blessed life is through Jesus Christ and the wonderful gift of the Holy Spirit. Here are a couple of my favorite encouraging verses for you:

Trust in the Lord with all your heart and lean not on your own understanding; in all your ways submit to him, and he will make your paths straight. (Proverbs 3:5-6)

Now may the God of peace, who through the blood of the eternal covenant brought back from the dead our Lord Jesus, that great Shepherd of the sheep, equip you with everything good for doing his will, and may he work in us what is pleasing to him, through Jesus Christ, to whom be glory for ever and ever. Amen. (Hebrews 13:20-21)

Tracy has been set ablaze by the power of the Holy Spirit. One of the main reasons we seek the baptism in the Holy Spirit is because He makes us bold and gives us more power to witness to others.

There is no doubt in my mind that Tracy is going to walk out of this jail and immediately begin doing the work of an evangelist. She has the heart of an evangelist. She longs to see God set others free from the grip of sin and addiction.

There's times when Tracy practically preaches my message before I can. The evidence of the Holy Spirit's work is absolutely undeniable in all these ladies' lives. I love seeing how He moves in power in their lives, and calls them to do miraculous things for God's glory.

I think back to when I was first set aflame by the power and infilling of the Holy Spirit. What a tremendous joy! I pray in tongues daily, and I believe it's only by His power that we are seeing these miraculous things happen in jails and prisons. Without having an intimate relationship with the Holy Spirit, I believe my ministry would be lacking.

I want to nurture my relationship with the Holy Spirit, so that I can always be usable for His purposes. It's not about what I hope to accomplish. It's about what He wants to accomplish through me. He leads, I follow.

Walking in Holiness

I remember when I was young, I wanted to go to the movie theater with my cousin. She attended regularly because her grandfather owned the theater. I remember asking my mother if I could go. Back then, you didn't go to a movie theater if you were a member of the Assemblies of God fellowship.

I remember clearly what my mom said after I had begged to go for about thirty minutes. She looked at me and said, "I guess you can go, but I sure hope Jesus doesn't come back while you're in there. He probably won't be looking for any Christians in the movie theater, and you'll probably get left behind."

Well, I went to the movies that night and watched the musical *Annie*. I will have to say that I was terrified the whole time that

Jesus would return and leave me in that theater. I was so relieved to see my mother drive up to get me after it was over. If she was still here, Jesus surely hadn't come back yet because He would have found her at home!

Our pastor preached on holiness and being set apart from the world. And though we may have taken a few things to an extreme back then, looking back now, I believe our lives truly would have been better without some of those things that we were told to stay away from. Compromise eventually led some of us down a slippery slope that has now become a devastating landslide of moral filth.

People don't want to talk about holiness much anymore. It's not a popular topic in the times we are living in. But we can't blame God for not moving in power today if we are not striving to live a life of holiness. God cleans up dirty vessels and uses them for His glory—I'm living proof of that. But He will not use dirty vessels who do not desire to be cleaned up and made usable.

I have seen a trend in a lot of pastors that has been very disturbing. Many pastors are surrendering to the influence of the world. Just this week alone, I saw a group of pastors arguing about whether or not it's okay to drink alcohol. I couldn't get over the number of pastors who were insisting there is nothing wrong with drinking socially. They began to refer to those of us who abstain as *legalistic*.

And as some began to speak of the devastating effects of alcohol on the body, their argument quickly turned to the sin of gluttony. That weak comparison seems to always rear its ugly head, and it infuriates me every time. Yes, we know gluttony is a sin. But, I've seen and heard of many innocent people killed by drunk drivers. To this day, I've never heard of one innocent person killed by someone who has had too many cheeseburgers.

I realize some people consider drinking to be a gray area. Having been delivered from alcohol myself, I know beyond a shadow of a doubt that consuming alcohol would be a sin for me. Honestly, I never did one single thing to glorify God while under the influence of alcohol, nor have I witnessed anyone else glorifying God while drinking.

But, even if I had never drunk alcohol and experienced its devastating effects, such as irresponsibility and depression, I wouldn't want to do anything that even had the remote possibility of making me unusable for God's glory. I have given myself away to Him for *His* purposes. If there are any gray areas, I choose to err on the side of caution. Why? Because more than anything else, I desire to walk in the power of the Holy Ghost. I long to see souls saved, and I will do whatever it takes to completely submit to God's plans. I do not want anything to hinder what God wants to do through me.

If I can't surrender something as trivial as a social drink, what else am I unwilling to surrender?

You see, I'm not special. I have no power of my own. That is obvious. I have no special talents, nor am I an eloquent theological speaker. But, I know what the power of God looks like on a life. I know what it *feels* like! I know that He can empower those who truly desire, more than anything else, to be usable for His glory.

Therefore, I don't want to do anything to grieve the Holy Spirit. He is my best friend. I don't want to offend Him. I love Him! I would be totally useless without His power. He leads me, teaches me, comforts me, empowers me, and *corrects me*—daily.

So my question to you is simply this: What kind of power do *you* want to walk in?

We don't like to talk about holiness much anymore. A lot of people have tried to pass holiness off as legalism. I know there are still some legalistic things out there to avoid today. But, I also know there is a huge deficit of holiness in this generation.

When did we shift from doing everything we could to please God to looking at everything we could "get away with" and still be considered a Christian? God hasn't changed; we have! If we want to see a genuine move of the Holy Spirit, God's going to need some genuine Christians to work with.

What kind of power do you want to walk in? What are you willing to give up so that you can be usable for His glory? There are some things that might not even be considered sinful that God wants you to walk away from. It's about being totally surrendered to His desires, not your own.

Instead of looking at what we can get away with, we must start looking at what we can get rid of in order to look more like Jesus. So, if you want to have a ministry that is alive with the power of the Holy Spirit, what are *you* willing to surrender?

I firmly believe there is a direct correlation between the amount of holiness we strive for and the amount of power we walk in. I've had to walk away from a lot of things to experience His power working through me—but I long to surrender even more, so that I can obtain more of His power!

I want to be a good steward of His presence so others can feel His power and expect something from God. I want others to be uplifted and encouraged to do more for God as well. We are in the *last* of the last days and there are so many lost people in the world headed for a devil's hell. We must be powered up to reach them and lead them to Jesus.

I speak this to you with as much love as I possibly can. We live in an hour where people need to see that God truly *is* who He says He is and that He still moves in power today. People need to know there is hope, and they need to know they, too, can walk in power.

Who will heed the call to be set apart? Who will desire holiness more than worldliness? Who will surrender all to walk in the power of the Holy Spirit?

> Then he said to them all, "Whoever wants to be my disciple must deny themselves and take up their cross daily and follow me." (Luke 9:23)

> Do not offer any part of yourself to sin as an instrument of wickedness, but rather offer yourselves to God as those who have been brought from death to life; and offer every part of yourself to him as an instrument of righteousness. (Romans 6:13)

> With this in mind, we constantly pray for you, that our God may make you worthy of your calling, and that by his power he may bring to fruition your every desire for goodness and your every deed prompted by faith. (2 Thessalonians 1:11)

I don't say anything of this to come off as judgmental. I want you to hear my heart in these words. I know the wonderful, inexpressible joy of being used by the Holy Spirit for God's glory. There is nothing more wonderful than seeing a soul set free or watching someone experience the powerful touch of God's hand through physical healing.

But we must walk in holiness. There seem to be some other trends appearing in some younger pastors who act and talk like the world in order to seem relevant, or in touch with the younger generation. It is having disastrous results.

My daughters told me about a youth pastor in a service they attended recently. He used expletives while interacting with them. One of my daughters said it made her feel uncomfortable because she felt he was trying to be cool in front of the young people present. But it backfired miserably. These young people made fun of him behind his back because he had just lost all respect in their eyes. It didn't make them think he was cool; it lessened his authority and equated him to just another worldly person.

They no longer took him seriously. They didn't see anything different in him than anyone else in the world. They had no interest in what he had to say from that point forward, choosing not to attend any more classes he offered. He also had no power. There was no anointing on his teaching, no conviction, nothing present to cause a young person to want to surrender to Christ.

A lack of holiness will always lead to a lack of power. And without the drawing power of the Holy Spirit, there is no catalyst for change.

Young people are surrounded by people who use bad language and curse constantly. We as leaders should be their safe place. We are called to be set apart. Most young people have had more than enough of what the world has to offer. They want to see someone they can look up to. How are they to believe they can abstain from sin if they have no earthly example?

They are looking for leaders that don't look or act like this world. They're looking for someone they can respect and aspire to be like. When we are not doing our best to look like Jesus, we are only hindering others from striving to be like Jesus.

When people see their leaders walking in the power and demonstration of the Holy Spirit, they will believe those same gifts are available to them. They will desire more from God and know the importance of walking in holiness. We are called to holiness. Why would we want to look like the world, when we have this most precious gift of salvation?

> But just as he who called you is holy, so be holy in all you do; for it is written: "Be holy, because I am holy." (1 Peter 1:15–16)

> But among you there must not be even a hint of sexual immorality, or of any kind of impurity, or of greed, because these are improper for God's holy people. Nor should there be obscenity, foolish talk or coarse joking, which are out of place, but rather thanksgiving. For of this you can be sure: No immoral, impure or greedy person—such a person is an idolater—has any inheritance in the kingdom of Christ and of God. (Ephesians 5:3–5)

I can only imagine what some of our jail services would look like if I went in there cursing like a sailor. Those men and women would take one look at me and wonder why I was trying to tell them what to do. My testimony would be destroyed. I can hardly bear the thought of it! I would look like the biggest hypocrite they had ever seen.

As I mentioned in a previous chapter about how the Holy Spirit helps us to walk in holiness, we read what James tells us about taming our tongues: "Out of the same mouth come praise and cursing. My brothers and sisters, this should not be. Can both fresh water and salt water flow from the same spring?" (James 3:10–11). How can we minister, or testify of God's goodness and grace if we turn around and begin to curse with the same tongue? I don't understand the benefit of using obscenities. I see none in it.

We must get back to sanctification and holiness. God expects more of us than just a lukewarm Christianity. Truly, I don't understand how anyone can continue walking in the ways of the world and call themselves a Christian with a clear conscience. If we are calling ourselves representatives of Christ Jesus, we had better be doing our best to look like Him.

One of the greatest deceptions our enemy is using in these last days is the idea that we must be, look, and act like the lost people we are trying to reach in order to effectively minister to them. What a pathetic lie. We must be set apart. We are called to be different. But, the enemy has convinced so many people that being different is not acceptable unless it is in a worldly manner.

Our society has chosen a type of nonconformity that has been pushed by a demonic agenda. Satan has ensnared so many to believe they need not conform to the sex or anatomy they were born with. He has deceived people into believing they can choose any identity they so desire.

Who ever imagined we would live in a world where some humans would identify as cats or dogs, or any other type of animal? If we had acted like this thirty years ago, we would have been locked up in a room with padded walls. But now anything goes, and it's celebrated instead of acknowledging it as perversion.

Satan will do anything he can to try and convince people to identify with the world rather than identify with the Creator who has made us in His own image.

So many who have been given the privilege of leading others out of the darkness somehow want to try to conform to the pattern that we see in the world. How does that lead anyone to freedom? The Word of God tells us not to be conformed to this world. "Do not conform to the pattern of this world, but be transformed by the renewing of your mind. Then you will be able to test and approve what God's will is—his good, pleasing and perfect will" (Romans 12:2).

How can we lead others to know what God's will is for their lives if we are not willing to stand out and allow the Holy Spirit to transform us before the eyes of those who are blinded by this world?

I'm not talking about a specific dress code, although I believe a Christian should dress modestly and decently. I'm not speaking of cutting or not cutting your hair if you're a female or of shaving or growing out your beard if you are a man. I'm talking about pursuing a lifestyle of holiness that is demonstrated in the way the world views us—nonconformity to this world!

Holiness should be seen in our actions, in our speech, in our attitudes, and in how we love and treat others. We can love sinners without joining them in sin. One blind man can't lead another blind man to a set destination. They will both be lost. Jesus spoke of blind guides leading the blind into a pit (Matthew 15:14).

But we are not blind.

The god of this age has blinded the minds of unbelievers, so that they cannot see the light of the gospel that displays the glory of Christ, who is the image of God. (2 Corinthians 4:4)

But whenever anyone turns to the Lord, the veil is taken away. (2 Corinthians 3:16)

We must walk in holiness if we intend to know the perfect and pleasing will of God. And we must not conform to this world if we want to lead others into a life of freedom and an eternity with Jesus Christ our Lord.

CHAPTER 6

Does God Trust You?

God's ways never cease to amaze me. We serve such a creative God that we could go to the utmost limits of our imaginations and still not be able to dream up some of the miraculous ways God can orchestrate things in our lives. Over the years, I've come to learn that we simply cannot put God in a box. He works in the simplest and most complex ways we could ever imagine!

When God first called me into ministry, I was visiting with a dear sweet lady who was also in ministry. She said something to me that I will never forget. It is a question I ask myself frequently to keep my focus on what I believe God is asking me to do for Him.

I had heard of a popular women's minister, Joani Tabor, and her thriving ministry. My mother had told me about this precious, powerful woman of God. I desperately wanted to hear her speak, but since she seemed to minister in many Southern states and I lived in Iowa at that time, I didn't think our paths would cross anytime soon.

But God works in mysterious ways. A few months after hearing of her ministry, God put her on my heart one day, out of the middle of nowhere. I had a strong feeling that I should contact her and simply pray for her. Of course I argued with God and told Him there was no way I could possibly do that. After all, I didn't even know how to get in touch with her.

After arguing with Him for a few hours, I looked her up on social media and sent her a message with a prayer that I had prayed for her. To my shock, she messaged me back almost immediately! She told me the prayer was so timely and meant so much to her.

She shared a bit of what she was going through, and I soon understood exactly why God had asked me to pray for her. A few weeks passed, and Joani messaged me and asked exactly where I lived in Iowa. She told me she had been invited to Iowa to speak at a women's conference. When I found out she would only be a couple of hours from me, I told her I would be there!

I didn't know at that time, but soon after I arrived, Joani shared with me that she needed me there that day. Because of what she was going through, she needed someone there as a support and encouragement to her. I never imagined she could possibly need *me* as a support for *her*!

As we sat together at lunch and talked, she spoke the words that impacted me more than anything she preached that day. She looked at me and said, "Donna, God trusts you, and that is no little thing! He knew He could count on you showing up here for me today, and that is the very reason He put me on your heart weeks ago. He knew He could send you, and you would come and be here with me. He trusts you!"

She had no idea what an impact those words would have on so many of the decisions I've made in my life and ministry since that day. How many times have I seen God move, and wondered why He would give me the honor of standing witness to the mighty things He has done? Then I would hear the echo of her words, *Because He trusts you, Donna!*

That is something I don't take lightly, and I strive to be more and more trustworthy every day so that God can use me for whatever purpose He should desire.

A couple of years ago, I had another amazing experience that once again reminded me of the importance of being found trustworthy by God. I hope I can put it into words as miraculously as it occurred.

Rev. David Wilkerson has always been one of my favorite evangelists. I've listened to his recorded sermons and read some of his books. I've always aspired to be a powerful and anointed evangelist like him and to always speak the truth with boldness like he did. He passed away in 2011, and I never had the opportunity to meet him or hear him speak in person. However, I was extremely blessed to meet and become friends with his niece, Julie Wilkerson Klose, a fellow author with Bridge Logos. And David's brother, Pastor Don Wilkerson, cofounder of Teen Challenge, blessed me tremendously by writing the foreword for my last book.

In 2019 just before Christmas, something incredibly unusual happened. I received a phone call from Des Moines, Iowa. I live in Tennessee now, but I get a lot of random calls from Iowa, so I assumed it was a telemarketer and didn't answer. A bit later I noticed the caller had left a voicemail message. I was shocked to hear these words on the other end of the line:

"Hi, this is Steven. I have a bit of an interesting story for you. I found a book on a park bench and didn't realize the meaning of it until I opened it and realized it is signed over to you from David Wilkerson, who is a famous evangelist. God told me to pick this book up personally. I found it on a park bench in Des Moines, Iowa, and I'd love to give it back, and maybe talk to you about a few things. I thought this was just amazing that I was told to pick this book up by God, and I would like you to contact me back."

I can't begin to tell you how puzzled I was. I've never had a book signed to me by Rev. David Wilkerson. And, honestly, if it had been any other author I probably wouldn't have even returned the call. I would have likely brushed it off as a wrong number. But curiosity got the best of me, and it wasn't long until I realized God was doing something miraculous.

When I called Steven back, we indeed discussed a few things. He told me that after he found the book, he looked up David Wilkerson on the internet and listened to some of his sermons. Then he looked me up and listened to some of my sermons. Seeing we were both evangelists, he assumed David Wilkerson had just signed the book and presented it to me as a friend. Little did Steven know, I had never met Rev. David Wilkerson.

As our conversation continued, it was obvious that Steven was looking for something more. As the Holy Spirit led me, I asked Steven if he wanted to give his heart to Jesus. In the next few moments Steven prayed and repented for his sins and rededicated his life to following Jesus as his Savior. What an amazing phone call this turned out to be!

Steven texted me a picture of the book, and sure enough, it was signed to Rev. Donna Sparks along with the date January 26, 2008. I know for sure I never met Rev. David Wilkerson, and he never signed a book for me.

I tried to figure out if there was any significance to the date Jan. 26, 2008. Well, the date is my mother's birthday, but 2008 was the year God called me to be an evangelist. I didn't even become *Reverend Donna Sparks* until 2014. Coincidence? Maybe.

I also wondered who this other Rev. Donna Sparks could be. And the more I thought about it, the more puzzling it seemed to become. I googled Rev. Donna Sparks, and the only one I could find was myself! This was surely a strange situation.

Don't get me wrong, I don't think the miracle in this story is that Rev. David Wilkerson signed a book to a lady named Rev. Donna Sparks in 2008. No, the miracle of this story is that God led a young man to a book on a park bench in Des Moines, Iowa, to learn of two evangelists—one of whom he was able to get in touch with. And when Jesus led him to me, I was able to lead Steven to Jesus in turn. Salvation is *always* the greatest miracle.

Steven sent me the book signed to *me* by David Wilkerson. As I looked at that simple weatherworn, water-damaged book that was left on a snowy park bench in Des Moines, I asked God why He would connect two people in such a way.

In the silence, I felt that sweet small voice of the Holy Spirit whisper, *Because I knew I could trust you to lead Steven to me.*

Oh how my heart leaped with joy! Once again, God had trusted me with someone who was precious to His heart. What an honor. I shared this story with many people over the past couple of years, and many have been blessed by how God will do some of the most amazing things to reach one treasured soul!

And God still wasn't done with the story. This past Christmas 2021, my pastor from my home church in Iowa, Westside Assembly in Davenport, invited me to come back and speak for the women's Christmas luncheon on Saturday and preach for the church service on Sunday morning. I'm always very thrilled to go back to Iowa, where we lived for almost nine years before God moved us back to Tennessee.

Soon after we arrived on Friday night, I felt a nudge from the Holy Spirit to contact Steven from Des Moines and invite him to church Sunday. "Des Moines is a three-hour drive from Davenport," I argued with God. "There's no way Steven would want to drive all the way to Davenport just for a Sunday morning service."

I couldn't push the thought out of my mind, though, so I searched my phone and sent him a text message. Exhausted from the long drive, I put my phone away and went to bed.

When I awoke the next morning, I was surprised to see that Steven had replied to my text message. He was excited to know I was in the state, and he would be coming to the service on Sunday. I think I squealed loud enough to wake my ministry partner, Sara, when I saw the message. I knew, once again, God was up to something!

The women's luncheon on Saturday was great. I decided to share the story of the mysterious book that was left on a snowy park bench in Des Moines, and how its discovery allowed me the honor of leading a young man to Jesus. I spoke of how God cares about all the tiny details of our lives and how He will orchestrate the miraculous to reach the one.

Sunday morning was a whirlwind, and I was greeting friends and acquaintances right up until the service started. I took my place on the front row as the worship team began to sing and lead us into the presence of God. My best friend, Ann, who is also my pastor's wife from Iowa, tapped me on the shoulder and told me to follow her.

She introduced me to Steven. He was there. I was so excited to meet this young man in person. What an awesome reminder of what God had done just two short years ago. He took a seat on the row of chairs behind me, and I soon went to the platform to begin my sermon.

The power and presence of the Holy Spirit was so thick in the church that morning. God was definitely there to do the miraculous. At the end of my sermon, I gave an altar call for salvation and rededication to Christ to which many people responded—praise God!

Then I gave an altar call for people who wanted to receive the baptism in the Holy Spirit. Several came forward, and Steven was one of them. I had the honor of praying with Steven, and he was filled to overflowing with the Holy Spirit and began to speak in tongues.

What a tremendous honor to once again see the hand of God move so sovereignly and powerfully in this young man's life. My pastor, Scott Rooks, invited Steven to join us for lunch, so we got to socialize a bit more before he headed back to Des Moines.

What lengths our God will go to in order to rescue us! I have no idea what wonderful plans our Father has for Steven. But, I know that He has chosen him, and set him apart for His very own purposes. What an amazing loving Father we have.

We sing the song, "Tis So Sweet to Trust in Jesus!" I can tell you from experience that it's just as sweet to know that Jesus trusts us! I'm continually humbled by all the lives Jesus has trusted me to speak into. It doesn't matter where I am. I can be in Walmart, jail, prison, or one of the finest churches in the nation. I don't care where, I simply hope to be found trustworthy, so that Jesus will allow me to be spectator of His life-giving mercy and grace.

How about you? Do you want to be the one He runs to when He needs someone to help rescue a lost soul? Do you want Him to trust you?

CHAPTER 7

Spiritual Discernment and Deception

One of the greatest gifts of the Holy Spirit is discernment. And oh, how desperately we need discernment in the day and age we live in. In my last book, *The Masquerade: Deception in the Last Days*, I shared a myriad of different ways Satan is using his influences to spread deception among even the *elect*. "For false messiahs and false prophets will appear and perform great signs and wonders to deceive, if possible, even the elect" (Matthew 24:24).

The baptism in the Holy Spirit helps us when it comes to different types of deception. It is alarming to see how easily people are being deceived in these last of the last days, but Jesus warned us of this.

One of the most destructive ways Satan is using deception today is through dividing God's children. I have always been very careful not to argue with people based on political views. I will say that I have very conservative views based on what I read in the Holy Bible. I try my best to be led by the Holy Spirit in all my decisions, political or other. That being said, I choose not to argue politics because I try my best to be a peacemaker.

Just to let you know in advance, this chapter is not about politics either. It's also not about COVID-19, and it's not about getting or not getting a vaccine, wearing or not wearing masks, bad cops, good cops, protesters, white privilege, Critical Race Theory, black lives matter, blue lives matter, racial or ethnic issues, violent protests, looting, or any of the thousands of other divisive topics flooding the media today.

But in essence it *is* about all of those things and more—and I'll tell you why. Regardless of what side you are on, the fact remains that there is a dividing line that causes us to choose sides. That dividing line has been perpetrated by Satan, who despises us no matter which side we are on.

All the division gets so very frustrating, and many of us feel so powerless to do anything about any of it in most cases. If we turn on the TV, we are bombarded by an agenda that propagates hate toward our fellow man. I don't care which side of the aisle you are on or what news network you are watching. I don't know about you, but fifteen minutes of watching can usually raise my blood pressure significantly.

One day in my frustration I called out to God and asked Him, "What are we supposed to do with this?" And as gently as He always does, He answered, *You can do exactly what you were called to do—you can love them anyway!*

As always, He was right. He always gives an answer that we can't argue with because His Word never changes.

We have been called to love our neighbors as ourselves, and we don't get the option to choose which neighbors. We simply must love. Nothing more and nothing less will make any kind of lasting impact. Consider what Jesus said when asked this question by the Pharisees.

"Teacher, which is the most important commandment in the law of Moses?"

Jesus replied, "'You must love the Lord your God with all your heart, all your soul, and all your mind.' This is the first and greatest commandment. A second is equally important: 'Love your neighbor as yourself.'" (Matthew 22:36–39 NLT)

We live in a fallen world, and trouble will always be present because of that. Everyone on planet Earth has problems of some kind. When frustrations arise accompanied by an air of injustice, people naturally want to lash out. However, there is not one single problem that can't be solved by following these two commandments: Love God, and love people.

But, this is the overall problem. We all have a common enemy. Maybe you don't believe Satan is real or that he exists, but he does. And he roams about "like a roaring lion looking for someone to devour" (1 Peter 5:8). He has been doing his evil work of trying to deceive and cause division between humanity from the day he first approached Eve in the garden.

His main goal is to separate people from God through sin and doubt. But think about this. As soon as Adam and Eve had eaten of the forbidden fruit the very first blame game started. When God called out to Adam and asked why he was hiding, Adam told God it was because he was naked. When God asked Adam how he knew he was naked, he blamed Eve for giving him the forbidden fruit. "The man said, 'The woman you put here with me—she gave me some fruit from the tree, and I ate it'" (Genesis 3:12).

But if we go back and look at Eve's conversation with the serpent, we see that Adam was with her. He was present during the whole discourse. "When the woman saw that the fruit of the tree was good for food and pleasing to the eye, and also desirable for gaining wisdom, she took some and ate it. She also gave some to her husband, *who was with her*, and he ate it" (Genesis 3:6 emphasis mine).

Satan initially brought forth deception by placing doubt in Eve's mind by asking, "Did God really say . . . ?" (Genesis 3:1). Then he sealed the deal with a lie that convinced her there would be no consequence for her disobedience when he said, "You will not surely die" (Genesis 3:4 NKJV).

That initial act of disobedience stole their innocence and gave sin entrance into their lives, immediately giving way to guilt and perpetrating blame in the heart of the very first human. Is it any wonder Satan has continued to use that same tactic for thousands of years?

But Jesus came and taught us how to forgive. He laid down His life for all of our sins knowing that many people would reject Him anyway. He demonstrated perfect love and unconditional forgiveness. And He asks us to love and forgive as well.

If everyone followed those two commandments I shared from the book of Matthew, there would be no division—no crime, no hate, no stealing, killing, or envy. Everyone would just love Jesus completely; therefore, there would be no sin. And if we loved each other as ourselves, we would always be concerned with making the lives of others better than our own. Sounds like heaven, doesn't it?

The sad truth is, heaven is the only place we will ever experience that kind of perfect society. We live in a fallen, imperfect world where Satan's one goal is to separate us from the One—Jesus—who loves us with a love that cannot be matched or even compared to. If he can cause us to hate one another, he ultimately separates us from God as well.

> Anyone who hates another brother or sister is really a murderer at heart. And you know that murderers don't have eternal life within them. (1 John 3:15 NLT)

> Whoever claims to love God yet hates a brother or sister is a liar. For whoever does not love their brother or sister, whom they have seen, cannot love God, whom they have not seen. (1 John 4:20)

Satan hates us because he will never be able to have what we will have with Jesus for eternity. He threw it all away because of pride and envy. Being filled with that kind of hatred, he has no ability to love, and his goal is to spread as much hate and division as he possibly can.

So let me ask you a rhetorical question. If you wanted to destroy the whole world and prevent people from going to heaven, what would you do? If I could even imagine being that evil my plan would probably look something like this.

First I would distract those Christians who do love God and put Him first. I would do everything within my power to get their eyes off Jesus, and I would flood their eyes and ears with the most negative, divisive propaganda I could possibly dream up.

I would use all media outlets, newspapers, Hollywood, and everything else I could find to spread my destructive agenda all over the world. I would use fear tactics to keep people upset and worried so they would continually turn on their TVs and tune into everything the media had to say.

I would make sure they opened their laptops, tablets, and smartphones and closed their Bibles. I would convince them that everything they saw or heard in the media was the unadulterated truth. I would keep them frustrated, hindered, and annoyed and cause them to forget what God's Word says:

> You will keep the mind that is dependent on You in perfect peace, for it is trusting in You. (Isaiah 26:3 HCSB)

> They will have no fear of bad news; their hearts are steadfast, trusting in the Lord. (Psalm 112:7)

> But he turned and said to Peter, "Get behind me, Satan! You are a hindrance to me. For you are not setting your mind on the things of God, but on the things of man." (Matthew 16:23 ESV)

Next I would do everything I could to divide people. I would use all my evil lies to bring in all kinds of offenses. I would try to promote a Babylonian mentality, causing people to be consumed with themselves. I would convince people to live their lives only for themselves because they *deserve* every good and extravagant thing they desire.

I would promote pride and arrogance fueled by materialism and covetousness. I would keep people focused on their personal achievements and what they could buy or own so they would begin to become envious and competitive toward one another. I would make sure they accumulated so much recreational *stuff*, they wouldn't have time to go to God's house.

I would cause people to be puffed up and consumed by the accolades of man. I would cause them to live for the praise of others. Using this tactic, I would wreak havoc in churches and on church platforms. Disunity would spread like wildfire, hindering the move of the Holy Spirit!

I would make sure people were easily offended and quick to hate. I would stir them to anger so they would be sure to take everything personally and consider no one else's feelings but their own. I would promote backbiting and speaking evil of others.

I would make sure people were consumed with feeding their fleshly desires. I would convince them that all sin is relative, and the Bible is hate speech. I would do my best to make them forget the sacrifice Jesus made for them and the prize He has promised to those who finish the race.

I would spread so much false information disguised as scientific facts and fuel so much hatred toward the Holy Bible that many would come to believe it was simply an irrelevant outdated book. And most importantly, I would convince church-going Christians that they should never say anything negative about sin so as not to offend anyone. I would make sure pastors never mentioned the reality of hell from the pulpit.

I would cause people to hate those who trust in God, and I would convince them that Christians are against them. Therefore, I would cause persecution against Christians to flourish. I would cause the voices of hate to become so loud and persuasive that Christians would cease to speak truth because of the fear of man.

Then when I finally had people distracted and divided against each other for every kind of reason, I would sit back and laugh as I continued to pour out even more deception than the world could imagine. I would introduce all kinds of false doctrines and heresies. I would send false prophets into churches so that even the elect would be deceived. I would do my best to twist every biblical truth I could. I would cause people to disrespect God in every way.

I would spread so much sin and perversion and cause people to become so trapped they would feel there was no hope of ever getting out. I would offer a myriad of empty promises as cures for their problems. I would make sure people were turning to drugs, alcohol, and sexual perversion as a means of escape from their pain. I would lie to them, convincing them that every sinful distraction is a means to escape.

Then I would convince them that their lives were worthless and meaningless. I would make sure they felt that no one cared or even noticed them. That would be pretty easy because very few *would* notice them—I'd have them focused on themselves, after all. I would convince them that they were completely hopeless with nowhere to turn, and I would make them think they had sinned too much to receive God's forgiveness. Then I would bring their sudden destruction.

Through all this, people would be so focused on the meaningless and temporary problems on earth—in this quickly vanishing vapor of life—they would have no expectation or anticipation of heaven and eternity with a loving God. They would not even notice the words of the Bible coming to life before their very eyes:

You should know this, Timothy, that in the last days there will be very difficult times. For people will love only themselves and their money. They will be boastful and proud, scoffing at God, disobedient to their parents, and ungrateful. They will consider nothing sacred. They will be unloving and unforgiving; they will slander others and have no self-control. They will be cruel and hate what is good. They will betray their friends, be reckless, be puffed up with pride, and love pleasure rather than God. They will act religious, but they will reject the power that could make them godly. Stay away from people like that! (2 Timothy 3:1–5)

I would create a smoke screen ensuring they would forget to watch for Christ's return, and I would keep them so upset over politics and other issues that they would talk about nothing else. I would make them forget that God is still in control. They would be so consumed with their own affairs that it would be just like it was in the days of Noah.

They wouldn't dare bother to share the gospel or attempt to rescue the lost and perishing. I would convince them that Jesus would not return in their lifetime, or ever. Then when Jesus does return, so many souls would be lost, and—by my evil logic—I would have won!

Satan is evil. His plans for us are evil.

This is why now more than ever before we must realize how important it is to be filled to overflowing with the Holy Spirit. Satan is clever. His tactics have worked to cause division for millennia. We must have discernment to see past his schemes so that we will not fall prey to his evil ways.

The Holy Spirit gives us discernment, and as we discussed before, He leads us into all truth. He guides us and directs us, and He makes it easier for us to love others. When we are armed with the power of the Holy Spirit, we will soon see that we are able to frustrate the plans of the enemy in our lives. We will be more focused on what the Spirit is directing us to do and His prompting us to minister to the needs of others rather than focusing on our own attainments.

We especially need the Holy Spirit to give us discernment when we are faced with blatant deception in the form of false prophets, or those who try to twist and pervert Scripture. The Holy Spirit helps us to know and remember what God's Word says so that we are not deceived.

The Holy Spirit draws us into communion with God. The world will always pull and tug at us with attempts to distract and drag us away from time in the Word of God and spending time in prayer. But the Holy Spirit woos us and draws us to the heart of God, and causes us to crave time in His presence. We will long to spend time praying in tongues, which strengthens us and refreshes us.

Our frustrations are lessened when we are revived and refreshed through the power of the Holy Spirit. Spending time with Him is like taking a vacation and temporarily leaving the problems of this world behind. But He gives us the added benefit of helping us to manage those frustrations through His power when they do come.

When it comes to human nature and human arguments, it doesn't matter who we might feel is right or wrong. We must realize that not everyone is going to agree with us all the time. Our way is not the only way. People can agree to disagree peacefully. But, *we are still required to love and forgive.* We must make a conscious decision to love, and the Holy Spirit will help us to do it when we make that decision.

I believe Jesus is coming soon. I believe we should examine our hearts and open our eyes. It's not time to become frustrated because of the problems in the world and give up, but we should stand strong determined to thwart all the plans of the enemy of our souls.

We can do this far more effectively if we are powered up, filled up, and on fire through the baptism in the Holy Spirit. Instead of giving way to distraction and division, let's keep our eyes on the cross, and our hearts tuned to the purpose we have been placed here for—the Great Commission:

> Therefore go and make disciples of all nations, baptizing them in the name of the Father and of the Son and of the Holy Spirit, and teaching them to obey everything I have commanded you. And surely I am with you always, to the very end of the age. (Matthew 28:19–20)

> Be careful, or your hearts will be weighed down with carousing, drunkenness and anxiety, and that day will close on you suddenly like a trap. For it will come on all those who live on the face of the whole earth. Be always on the watch, and pray that you may be able to escape all that is about to happen, and that you may be able to stand before the Son of Man. (Luke 21:34–36)

CHAPTER 8

Walking in the Anointing

Growing up, I can recall many people talking about the anointing. I heard phrases like *Our pastor certainly is anointed* or *You sure could feel the anointing on that sermon.* I've also heard things like *Well, he's a pretty good teacher, but he's just not anointed* or *When she sang and played the piano the anointing was all over her!*

But, what exactly is *the anointing*? It is such an elusive thing but feels very tangible at times as well. It's hard to put into words exactly. It is so obvious when it's present, yet equally evident when it's absent. It sounds like a riddle, doesn't it?

Merriam-Webster defines the verb **anoint** as:

1. to smear or rub with oil or an oily substance
2. **a:** to choose by or as if by divine election

b: to designate as if by a ritual anointment[5]

We most often think back to the Old Testament of the Bible when kings were often anointed with oil to designate their appointment to that position. I most frequently think of David when he was anointed as king:

> Then Jesse told his son Abinadab to step forward and walk in front of Samuel. But Samuel said, "This is not the one the Lord has chosen." Next Jesse summoned Shimea, but Samuel said, "Neither is this the one the Lord has chosen." In the same way, all seven of Jesse's sons were presented to Samuel. But Samuel said to Jesse, "The Lord has not chosen any of these." Then Samuel asked, "Are these all the sons you have?"
>
> "There is still the youngest," Jesse replied. "But he is out in the fields watching the sheep and goats."
>
> "Send for him at once," Samuel said. "We will not sit down to eat until he arrives."
>
> So Jesse sent for him and had him brought in. He was dark and handsome with beautiful eyes.
>
> And the Lord said, "This is the one; anoint him."
>
> So as David stood there among his brothers, Samuel took the flask of olive oil he had brought and anointed David with the oil. And the Spirit of the Lord came powerfully upon David from that day on. Then Samuel returned to Ramah. (1 Samuel 16:8–13)

In this case we can see that God was appointing David for service as king. It was demonstrated outwardly through Samuel pouring a horn of oil over his head. Anointing in this way meant that something was set apart for God's use, sacred, or consecrated for His service. The items and furnishings in the tabernacle were also anointed with oil.

The oil has always represented the Spirit of God, and we can see here that the Scripture says, "From that day on the Spirit of the Lord came powerfully upon David."

David was *designated* as king through the physical application of oil. But he was given special power, wisdom, strength, and abilities beyond what he could normally accomplish on his own through the power of the Holy Spirit. There was something *different* about him. He now had the anointing, and it was evident to others. Not the anointing as in the appointing as king—that wouldn't be made known until several years later—but something indescribable yet still obvious.

Here's what Saul's attendant said about David: "One of the servants answered, 'I have seen a son of Jesse of Bethlehem who knows how to play the lyre. He is a brave man and a warrior. He speaks well and is a fine-looking man. And the Lord is with him'" (1 Samuel 16:18).

Saul was being tormented by an evil spirit, and he needed someone who could play the lyre to calm him. David had been anointed to play the lyre. He was good at it no doubt, but there was something more, something that brought relief to Saul and comforted him. It was the anointing.

When talking about anointing with oil, we know that it is also used when we pray for the sick. Once again, the oil is representative of the Holy Spirit's power. In the New Testament, the disciples anointed the sick as Jesus had taught them. "They drove out many demons and anointed many sick people with oil and healed them" (Mark 6:13). James also tells us to anoint the sick with oil and pray for them. "Is anyone among you sick? Let them call the elders of the church to pray over them and anoint them with oil in the name of the Lord. And the prayer offered in faith will make the sick person well" (James 5:14–15).

But when I refer to walking in the anointing, I think about what happened when Jesus was anointed. "You know what has happened throughout the province of Judea, beginning in Galilee after the baptism that John preached—how God anointed Jesus of Nazareth with the Holy Spirit and power, and how he went around doing good and healing all who were under the power of the devil, because God was with him" (Acts 10:37–38).

When Jesus was baptized by John, He was then anointed with the Holy Spirit and power. He went around doing good and healing because God was with Him. The anointing gives evidence that God is with us, working through us. We see evidence of this in Luke:

> He went to Nazareth, where he had been brought up, and on the Sabbath day he went into the synagogue, as was his custom. He entered the synagogue on the Sabbath. And when He stood up to read, and the scroll of the prophet Isaiah was handed to him. Unrolling it, he found the place where it was written:
>
> "The Spirit of the Lord is on me,
>   because He has anointed me
>   to proclaim good news to the poor.
> He has sent me to proclaim freedom for the prisoners
>   and recovery of sight for the blind,
> to set the oppressed free,
>   to proclaim the year of the Lord's favor."

Then he rolled up the scroll, gave it back to the attendant, and sat down. The eyes of everyone in the synagogue were fastened on him. He began by saying, "Today this Scripture is fulfilled in your hearing." All spoke well of him and were amazed at the gracious words that came from his lips. (Luke 4:16–22)

Once again we can see what the anointing does by Jesus confirming, "The Spirit of the Lord is on Me, because He has *anointed* Me . . ."

I love reading about some of the old-time evangelists—those who had amazing and miraculous ministries. I think of men like Smith Wigglesworth, who had such a powerful anointing from the Holy Spirit that almost everyone he prayed for received physical healing. He even raised around twenty people from the dead!

One of my favorite healing evangelists was Kathryn Kuhlman. Though she is deceased now, when I listen to recordings of her speaking, they bring me to tears to this very day. There's something about the anointing that she carried. People were miraculously healed in her services, and she rarely laid a hand on any of them before they were healed. She often prayed for the individuals after they had received their healing, and the power of the Holy Spirit was so strong on her that people would fall to the floor under the power of the Holy Spirit. She rarely preached long, eloquent messages, but you could feel the Holy Spirit's anointing on every single word.

I never got to be in one of her services, but I've read countless testimonies where people described the atmosphere as feeling like it was charged with electricity. Her relationship with the Holy Spirit was so intimate, and she handled that relationship as if it were such a fragile thing—a precious gift. She always worried about offending the Holy Spirit. She never wanted to do anything to grieve Him. She was always so careful to give God all the glory for every thing He did. She knew she could do nothing within herself, but because of her devout friendship with the Holy Spirit, she knew she could trust Him to anoint her and do the miraculous through her.

Oh how desperately we need more people today who would become so hungry for the Holy Spirit, and would handle Him with such care as to not grieve Him in any way. I truly feel we would see Him do those things and so much more again.

I believe He wants to perform miracles in a greater magnitude than we have ever seen before. But how can He do those things when so many of us are seeking to make a name for ourselves? How many of us will actually move out of His way and steward an atmosphere for God's glory to be revealed?

Kathryn Kuhlman was such a great steward of the presence of God. She was selfless, and she surrounded herself with others who put God on a pedestal, not themselves. She didn't want anyone to even come close to praising her for what happened in her services. The glory was God's alone, and she made sure everyone knew it.

Oh how I long for those days again! My heart breaks because of how the enemy of our souls has blinded us with pride, comparison, and competition though we are all supposed to be on the same team. He has really wreaked havoc in the church universal, making many powerless and dry.

There are so many lifeless churches today. It's almost as if you want to check for a pulse when you enter the door. Oh, they may be singing loud and have the most talented singers and musicians, but there's no anointing. There may be bright flashing lights and fog machines but no evidence of the Holy Spirit being present. There may be a very charismatic and well-spoken minister behind the pulpit but no conviction or persuasion to repent of sin. There may be every kind of program or small group available to attend but no encouragement to go out and fulfill the Great Commission. There may be all kinds of activities, fun, and games but no baptisms in the Holy Spirit, no intercession, and no weeping over the lost.

Where is the preaching of the good news and the proclamation of freedom for the captives? Where can people go to receive healing—sight for the blind—and deliverance for the oppressed? Where are the churches where people are truly walking in the anointing of the Holy Spirit?

We need men and women who are so hungry and thirsty for the things of God that they dare not dream of stepping on a platform without praying heaven down. We need hearts that are so cautious and careful not to grieve the Holy Spirit that He can actually use us to do the miraculous without getting puffed up in ourselves.

Oh that we could rid ourselves of every selfish motive and surrender completely to the work of the Holy Spirit—not to be seen or heard, or praised but to truly bring forth miracles to lives that are desperate. That we would strive to be the living examples this world desperately needs to believe that God is still God.

I believe we can get back there again. I believe we can walk in the anointing. It's not something we can earn, and it's not something that can be learned. It must come from a close and serious relationship with the Holy Spirit. It must be cultivated and nourished with an undivided heart.

It comes only through spending time with Him. I make a point to pray in tongues daily. I never get up to speak to a group, big or small, without seeking God with my whole heart and praying in the Holy Spirit. I know that I have no power of my own. But I know the amazing power He has!

I also know that the words I speak will hold no conviction, no sway, and no hope unless the Holy Spirit anoints me to speak those words. I know what it's like to have the anointing and feel Him empowering me to speak or pray with someone. I also know what it's like to try to do it on my own, and I know how terrible that goes.

It's a terrible thing to get up to speak and feel as if the anointing has been withdrawn from you. I could not continue in ministry if I felt that very often. I dare not do anything without the guidance and leadership of the Holy Spirit. Yet some people have become quite accustomed to it, sadly.

For myself, trying to do anything without the empowerment of the Holy Spirit is only setting me up to fall flat on my face. More than anything in this world, I long to feel Him equipping me to do whatever He is leading me to do. I don't need man's praise or compliments. I simply live for that nod of approval I feel from the Holy Spirit when I've followed Him in total trust and obedience.

I can never get enough of the Holy Spirit. I can never be close enough to Him. I always thirst for more. The amazing thing is, we can go deeper and deeper with Him. He has so much more to offer and lead us into. Like I said before, I admire the old-time evangelists. One day I will meet them and ask them all kinds of questions.

But I don't want to be the next Kathryn Kuhlman. I don't want to be the next Aimee Semple McPherson, or Maria Woodworth Etter. Although I admire their ministries and the wonderful works they achieved, I wouldn't want to be them. No, I don't want the relationship they had with the Holy Spirit, and I don't desire the ministry of anyone alive today either.

I want the privilege of growing in, nurturing, and cherishing my own relationship with the Holy Spirit. I want to do the things He has planned for *me* to do. Great or small, if He leads me to do it for God's glory, it will be enough for me.

What kind of anointing do you want on your life? Are you content with where you are, or do you desire a deeper, more intimate relationship with the Holy Spirit? There's nothing like leaning on Him, trusting Him, and being empowered by Him.

Start working on a deeper, richer relationship with Him today. Think about Him. What grieves Him? What pushes Him away? What draws Him to us? Do we see our relationship with Him as a precious and fragile gift? Or is it something we rarely think about? Do we strive to include Him in every aspect of our lives, or is He only an afterthought or a Sunday morning friend?

We can have as much of the Holy Spirit or as little of Him as we desire. Can we be honest about our motives and truly die to self in order to give Him complete freedom and liberty within us?

Loved one, He longs to use you! Let us foster an atmosphere where He has freedom to do the miraculous!

CHAPTER 9

Walking in Compassion

Rev. Scott Rooks began his ministry as an evangelist, and his heart for evangelism still drives him to this day. As my pastor at Westside Assembly in Davenport, Iowa, he became a mentor to me and helped me acquire my credentials as a minister with the Assemblies of God. He also became my friend. His wife, Ann, has become my best friend, and we keep in touch though the miles have separated us. I have tremendous respect for both of them.

They have the tenderest hearts for the lost and broken. They have demonstrated this compassion in many ways, but one instance sticks out in my mind more than the others.

One Sunday morning Pastor Scott was preaching, and might have been halfway through his message, when a rather tall, muscular man got out of his seat and came barreling down the aisle toward the platform. By the look in this man's eyes and his demeanor, I was certain that he was going to punch Pastor Scott in the face. He looked like a giant compared to my pastor, and I was afraid this was going to go very badly.

To my surprise, Pastor Scott came down the stairs and off the platform so fast it made my head spin. He ran to this man with arms outstretched and hugged him with all his might. The man began to weep, and Pastor Scott knelt with him and led him to Jesus right then and there. I could only cry.

I have recalled that Sunday many times over, and I have wondered how many pastors would have called for security, or asked for someone in the congregation to deal with him. And I'm sure most people wouldn't have blamed him if he had done so.

But there was a deep compassion in my pastor that overwhelmed his heart with mercy, and compelled him to meet this sinner on his way to the altar. It reminded me of the parable of the prodigal son. Pastor Scott welcomed and led this wayward son back into the arms of a loving and gracious Savior—Jesus Christ.

Pastor Scott has preached many wonderful sermons, but that one demonstration of compassion spoke louder than any words he has ever uttered.

Compassion is contagious. The closer we get to Jesus, the more we start to have a heart like His. When we are moved with compassion for the lost, we see the utmost importance in leading them to Jesus so they can experience freedom and peace and ultimately an eternity in Heaven with Him.

Love and compassion also open the door for the miraculous. How many times in the New Testament do we read of how

Jesus was moved with compassion for the sick and afflicted? Here are three:

> When Jesus landed and saw a large crowd, he had compassion on them and healed their sick. (Matthew 14:14)

> Jesus had compassion on them and touched their eyes. Immediately they received their sight and followed Him. (Matthew 20:34)

> Jesus called his disciples to him and said, "I have compassion for these people; they have already been with me three days and have nothing to eat. I do not want to send them away hungry, or they may collapse on the way." (Matthew 15:32)

In a world so filled with hatred, it is hard to have compassion for some people. It's especially difficult if they are cursing our God, and speaking terrible things about Him. So often we want to retaliate. It's in our human nature to become angry and want to strike back, even though we know we should turn the other cheek.

One day I was feeling extremely angry over some posts I had read on social media. People were saying all kinds of evil things about God. They were making fun of Him, calling Him terrible names, and denying His existence. I typed up a whole post with a fiery passion to set them straight. The Holy Spirit stopped me before I could submit it and made me delete it.

"But God," I whined, "I'm only trying to defend You!"

At that very moment, and as clear as day, He replied, "I never asked you to defend me; I asked you to represent me."

Ouch! That hit hard.

If I'm His representative, I'd better be acting and looking like Him, not arguing with people who are probably not going to listen to me anyway. And if I'm going to open my mouth, what comes out better be flowing with compassion. That is so hard sometimes. But if we want to see God move in our lives and ministries we must learn to walk in compassion. The only way to do that is to let Jesus love people through us.

I've often had opportunities while ministering in the jails to act on and demonstrate the ability to love like Jesus. I've rarely had trouble with many of the ladies in the jail, but a few years ago I had one inmate who was determined to make my life a living nightmare. She came into the service cursing and being extremely disrespectful. She would not listen to me and was a tremendous distraction to everyone else.

The ladies would ask her to be quiet and stop cursing because she was being disrespectful and hateful. She shouted, "I don't give a [expletive]!" I really wanted to have her thrown out. I have the option to ask the correctional officers to come and get disruptive inmates and take them back to their pods at any time. But if they are taken out of the service they are not allowed to come back.

My patience was growing thin, and I was just before calling them to come and get her. But inside I knew the Holy Spirit was not releasing me to do so. I bit my tongue and tried to ignore her shenanigans. The following week I was filled with dread when I saw her walk into the room again. Once again I endured her disruptions, and I allowed her to stay in the service even though I desperately wanted to kick her out.

She repeated her performance again—disruptive, rude, obnoxious, argumentative, and using all manner of profanity. I was so close to calling the jailers, but once again I felt that I needed to endure. I admit, I was finding it very hard to love this one. She was making ministry extremely difficult, but God was still obviously working in the lives of the other ladies.

On the third week I had determined that if she came to the service and repeated her performance, I was going to have her permanently removed. Once again, she waltzed in the door and continued her tirade of profanity and blatant dismissal of everything I said. I was beginning to have very bad feelings toward this lady—very bad.

I realized there was no way I could love her on my own. I began to pray for her, and I began to ask God to please help me love her. She was so rude to me and so disrespectful to Him; I could hardly stand it anymore. I couldn't understand why the Holy Spirit simply wouldn't allow me to have her removed. But the more I prayed for her, the more I began to sense His peace and a deep stirring of compassion in my heart toward her.

The following week when I went into the jail, I still had the feeling of dread when I saw her come into the room. I felt like every word I had spoken for the past four weeks had gone in one ear and out the other as far as she was concerned. There were a few new ladies in the service, and after I opened with prayer we went into the praise and worship service. Some of the ladies requested to sing "Redeemed" by Big Daddy Weave.

As we sang those words, many of the ladies were crying, and others had their hands raised and were rejoicing. When the song was over, I said, "Some of you sang that song with great joy because you have experienced God's redeeming love and forgiveness. But some of you are longing to be able to sing that song and truly mean it."

The Holy Spirit's presence was so evident and so overwhelming in the room at that moment. I continued to let the Holy Spirit speak through me and ended with an altar call. Four more ladies gave their hearts to Christ, and there was great rejoicing!

I asked if they wanted to sing the song again now that they could sing it truthfully and from the heart. The ladies gave me a resounding "Yes!" As we began to sing it again, I walked around the room hugging each one of them and telling them how proud I was of them.

When I approached "little Miss Disruptive," I looked at her and was suddenly overwhelmed with compassion for her. Tears rolled down her face. When I neared her, she grabbed me and began to weep uncontrollably. She said, "I am so, so, sorry, Miss Donna. Will you please forgive me?"

I was crying too as I said, "Yes, dear, of course I forgive you. I come to this jail because I love you, and I believe in you. You really frustrated me, but I still love you and want the best for you. I want to see you set free and living the life God has planned for you!"

She continued to weep as she hugged me and would not let go. She apologized over and over again. In the next few moments, I led her to Christ, and as we continued to sing "Redeemed," she had the biggest, most beautiful smile on her face. Both hands were raised to heaven as tears dripped onto her orange jumpsuit.

The ladies who had seen the ugly side of her began to walk over and hug her as well. It was an incredible service. God's love poured into that room in the most powerful way. All the irritation, frustration, and anger seemed to just dissolve away as each one approached her and embraced her. The following week was peaceful, and she was so well behaved. It was a miracle as far as I was concerned.

The next week I found out she had been released, and I thought about how that situation could have taken a totally different turn if I had kicked her out. If I had kicked her out, she would have left that jail without coming to Jesus. Even though I couldn't see it on the outside, Jesus was working on her on the inside.

I was reminded of how quick we are to write someone off when they disappoint us or cause us frustration. I also remembered something I have said to others so many times—"Hurting people hurt people. But I believe that freed people free people." We must sometimes pray for patience and allow the Holy Spirit to guide us so we can be people who help free hurting people. It's not easy to love the unlovable, but when we allow Jesus to love them through us, He makes it possible.

As we continue to walk in compassion, we will see God move in more powerful ways in our lives. I believe our love and compassion for people moves God's heart and causes Him to reach down and heal people physically as well as emotionally and spiritually.

It's easy for us to succumb to anger and desire to give people a piece of our minds. But we simply can't see the whole picture. God *does* see the whole picture. He knows what He is doing in a life when all we see are the hateful actions and attitudes of those who try to push us away.

Another side of the coin is forgiveness. We must also be willing to forgive so that we *can* love. We long to see God do the miraculous, and we long to walk in His immeasurable power. But if we can't forgive others when they offend us or hurt us, how can we expect God to trust us with His power?

Jesus endured humiliation and suffering like we will never know even though He lived a perfect, sinless life. None of us are perfect. We can never attain the perfection Jesus walked in. We are human. But so many times we expect others to be perfect in order to gain our forgiveness or compassion. How can we be forgiven if we are not willing to forgive? "For if you forgive other people when they sin against you, your heavenly Father will also forgive you. But if you do not forgive others their sins, your Father will not forgive your sins" Matthew 6:14–15.

If we are not walking in love and forgiveness, how can we expect to walk in His power? We must make ourselves usable for His glory. That involves doing some hard things like forgiving and loving the unforgivable.

Early in my ministry there was someone dear to me who hurt me severely. She had said some things about me behind my back that cut me to the core. I couldn't believe she could be so loving and gracious to me when we were together but was so hurtful and vengeful when she spoke about me to others.

I wanted to hold onto the hurt. I wanted to be mad at her and let her know I was mad. I certainly didn't want to forgive her and give her the satisfaction of feeling like it was okay. But soon God began to reveal to me that His desire was to lead me into deeper waters. He wanted to empower me to do more and be able to minister more effectively.

But to go with God, you have to travel light. There is no room for excess baggage. I had to let go of the offense, hurt feelings, and unforgiveness if I was going to go anywhere! So I made a decision to forgive. It wasn't easy. But when I decided that I was going to do the opposite of what my flesh desired, I began to feel a love and compassion for my friend that I had never felt.

The enemy wanted me to coddle the hurt feelings and nurture the offense. He knew if he could make me dwell on those things, I would be stuck. I wouldn't be able to progress in the things God was calling me to do. I had to decide which was more important to me. Was it more important to be mad and offended, or was it more important to forgive and let God mold me into His image?

We have to realize when we are struggling to have love and compassion for others, whether it is due to their actions or attitudes, it is only a trap. Oh how sneaky Satan is! He plays off our human nature so well. He recognizes the weakness of our flesh and encourages us to feed the flesh rather than move with the Spirit.

But when we realize what a great price Jesus paid to bring us freedom, how can we withhold forgiveness from others and hinder the plans He has had for us from the beginning?

Everyone needs love and compassion. We all need to receive it freely and give it freely. When we let go of the weights of offense that keep us stuck on the ground, we will soon lift off and begin to see God do the miracles in and through our laid down lives.

God loves to see His children walking in compassion just as we love to see our own children getting along and loving one another. How much more do you think our Heavenly Father loves to see His children walking in compassion?

CHAPTER 10

Listen Before You Leap

I firmly believe God is calling many of us to step out of our comfort zones and into miracle zones. In fact, the step He's asking you to take may feel more like a giant leap. It may sound scary or impossible to you. But God has done the impossible over and over again throughout history—and He usually does it with ordinary, unsuspecting people! I can certainly attest to the fact that He has been calling me to leap a lot recently. It has been anything but comfortable, but it has been so worth it!

When I received a message from a prison chaplain asking me to come and minister to the men who were incarcerated in his prison, I experienced a whole gamut of emotions. It sounded exciting but also terrifying. I'm completely comfortable ministering in female jails and prisons, but going into a men's prison was a totally different story.

And believe me, I've heard stories. My mentor shared his experience of going into men's prisons only to find they were only interested in him long enough to find out if he had postage stamps. Another individual told me stories of angry and hateful men who only wanted to argue and make fun of God. Others told me stories of violent men who would try to harass me as a female, and they tried to convince me it was far too dangerous for a female to even consider.

My husband wasn't exactly thrilled with the idea himself. But knowing my heart for ministry to the lost and broken, he reluctantly agreed to let me go and gave me his blessing. After jokingly saying, "Well, it was nice knowing you!"

There was one more obstacle; I needed a ministry partner to go with me. Unfortunately most of my ministry team has dissipated for various reasons during the months of COVID-19 lockdowns. Completely out of the blue, God sent Sara to help me. I'll be the first to admit—and I'm sure she agrees—that she was probably the least likely to help me. Sara is very quiet and shy, and I knew before I asked her that this would be way beyond her comfort zone. I anticipated a great big *No!*

Amazingly, she agreed to go with me, and God is using her powerfully! Little did I know that God had already been dealing with her to step out of *her* comfort zone. He had been speaking, and she had been listening, so she took the leap!

Sara and I went to the prison and took the training class. When we arrived at the ominous, looming prison that serves as home to over 1,500 male inmates, we both took a deep breath. Then we looked at each other and said at the same time, "What have we gotten ourselves into?" Still, we mustered up our courage and headed for the front gate.

We made our way through security where all our belongings, including our own bodies passed through X-ray. Then we were patted down to make sure we hadn't brought in anything. Finally we were inside all the gates. The chaplain led us to the visitation gallery because the number of men signed up for our church service wouldn't fit in the chapel where services are normally held. We quickly set up the projector and speaker and made sure everything was working.

I had been battling a cold and sinus infection for over a week and was still having trouble speaking without having a major coughing attack. That was what I was worried about more than anything. I had perfect peace about ministering to these men, but my biggest fear was losing my voice! Sara also said she felt completely at ease and had no fear. That's God!

The buzzer sounded, and in walked the chaplain with a large group of male inmates. I was completely overwhelmed by the peace and calm I felt. When God calls us to a task, He equips and empowers us for it. I had no fear because I was certain that He had opened this door for us. The Holy Spirit was with me, and He was leading and directing the entire event. I only needed to be submissive to His plans.

I asked those men if they were ready for revival. They responded with a resounding "Yes!" I knew at that moment God was going to do the miraculous. We sang a couple of songs, and I began to share the message God had put on my heart. That's when my greatest fear was realized. I lost my voice! I couldn't speak a word without coughing. Cough drops were not working! I asked the chaplain for some water, and he, hesitantly, had to leave us all alone with the inmates to go get water.

Finally, I was able to speak again. But that was also my cue from the Holy Spirit to end it. I had said enough. Now it was time to get out of the way and allow Him to do what He does best. I gave an invitation for salvation, and almost all those men raised their hands. I led them in a prayer for salvation. Then we went back into worship, and I told them to come forward if they needed prayer for specific needs. One by one the men came forward for prayer as the worship music played.

There was an older gentleman who was shaking uncontrollably because he suffered from Parkinson's disease. He wanted me to pray for his healing. I began to pray for him, but God stopped me. He told me to ask the man if he wanted to be baptized in the Holy Spirit. When I asked, the man replied, "Yes!" I prayed for him, and Jesus baptized him in the Holy Spirit with the evidence of speaking in tongues. Soon after that he completely stopped shaking. The chaplain told me that he believed he was healed because he had never seen him stop shaking.

Two more men were baptized in the Holy Spirit with the evidence of speaking in tongues, and many others came forward for healing and prayers for their families. God was moving in power! It was the most beautiful thing to see. The men thanked us repeatedly for coming, and we told them we would be back next month.

I think I floated out of the prison that day. When I got home, I was recalling every thing God had done in the service. I remembered the man who was healed from Parkinson's disease. Then I remembered how God stopped me and asked me to ask the man if he wanted to be baptized in the Holy Spirit before He healed him, and I asked Him why He did it that way.

I heard His tender voice say these words to me: "If a person can have faith to believe for their salvation, then they surely have faith to believe for the baptism in the Holy Spirit. And if a person can believe for and experience the wonderful supernatural gift of receiving the Holy Spirit and speaking in tongues, how much more will they be able to believe for their healing?"

Wow! I couldn't believe it. How true that was! When we have the faith to believe for salvation, we can also believe for the gift of the Holy Spirit, but when we have received this precious gift, how much more faith do we have to take that leap of faith for our healing? God knew exactly what this man needed.

It's not always easy to take a leap of faith, but if God is calling us to do something for Him, the Holy Spirit will definitely come alongside us to help us do those things. There's a popular adage that I've heard many people quote: "Fake it till you make it!" I hate that little phrase because we don't have to fake anything where God is involved.

The Holy Spirit empowers us with the real thing! That's not to say you won't ever have any issues or make any mistakes. There will always be a learning curve, but when we simply allow the Holy Spirit to teach us, and we take that leap of faith, He's going to be there.

I remember the very first time I was ever asked to speak for an event. I didn't have any ministerial credentials, and I was very unsure of this calling. In fact, I spent most of my time in the ladies' restroom before I got up to speak. I was so nervous I was sure I was going to lose my lunch in front of everyone. But, I wanted to do this more than anything in the world. God had placed a burning desire in my heart to share the gospel.

I stood behind that podium hoping no one would be able to tell how nervous I was. I had prayed all week asking God to give me the right message and to allow me to speak it boldly. And He did! One of my friends approached me after the service and said, "Wow! I had no idea you could preach like that!"

I looked at her and said, "Neither did I." I honestly think I was more shocked than anyone in that place.

As I drove home that night, I was on cloud nine. I simply could not believe the anointing and calm that I felt as I preached. Shortly after that, my pastor asked me to preach for our Sunday morning service. I studied, and prayed, and studied and prayed some more. I was nervous again, but I felt the Holy Spirit would help me again.

I wanted to come up with an impressive sermon with lots of Scripture. I wanted to sound really smart. I was really going to impress my church family, especially since it had gone so well the last time I spoke. Well, guess what? It was horrible. I absolutely tanked that morning. I could tell. People were bored, and all that material I had typed up to share seemed to go in one ear and out the other. It was so bad, even I was bored! My pastor gave me some constructive feedback after the service, which was appreciated but made me feel even worse.

How could it have gone so well the first time I spoke and tanked so miserably the very next time? Because I assumed too much. I had taken a leap, but I didn't allow the Holy Spirit to lead me this time. I thought I could come up with an impressive message that would really impact the hearers. But I was so wrong.

I'm so glad God let me fall on my face that morning.

It was painful at the time, but it taught me one of the most valuable lessons I've ever learned. It's great to take a leap into the unknown, but make sure you are holding hands with the Holy Spirit when you do! Listen carefully before you leap. Allow Him to lead, and you follow. Even if the message seems simplistic, and you feel you can make a bigger impact by doing things your way, remember He knows best! Our human wisdom is garbage compared to the knowledge of God.

He knows who He is sending you to. He knows their struggles, their pain, and everything that is going on inside them. No matter how hard we try, we cannot know what the Holy Spirit intends to do in every life. So, if we take a leap without holding tightly to Him, we will be wandering around in the dark with no sense of direction. And that is a terrible feeling.

When God began to use me in the prophetic, I was terrified. I've never wanted to say anything that is not from God! This felt like I was taking a huge leap all over again. The very first time God spoke to my heart and asked me to share something with someone, I was extremely hesitant. I was praying with a young lady at the altar when I clearly heard the Holy Spirit whisper to me, "Tell her now is not the time to shrink back."

I didn't know anything about this young lady. I didn't know what her situation was or anything else about her. But I knew I should tell her what God had spoken to me. Reluctantly, I opened my mouth to tell her, and after I had spoken those words, she started crying uncontrollably. I was shocked. After I finished praying with her, she told me just how significant those words were to her.

She was in college and had been very bold with her faith. But due to some situations she had encountered and being around some of the influences she was in contact with, she had become less vocal. She said she felt herself slipping, and she hated feeling like she was becoming weak and stagnant. Those words were the exact words she had been thinking when I came over and prayed for her. It was a confirmation to her that God was telling her not to run, but to stand!

The next time God led me to speak a word to someone was when I was preaching at a church in Mississippi. Several responded to the altar call. When I approached one of the ladies at the altar, the Holy Spirit put it on my heart to tell her she was called to preach. Once again, I knew nothing about this lady. I had never seen her before in my life. It took a leap of faith to speak those words to her. But I did, and she started weeping.

Today she is in ministry and is preaching the gospel. She told me she might never have believed that God wanted to use her if it hadn't been for the words He had me speak to her that day. How important it is that we listen for the precious voice of the Holy Spirit and then dare to take a leap and speak it out in faith.

There may be times that we miss the mark and fall on our face. But God is faithful, and He will help us when we strive to do what He asks us to do. Don't doubt His plans.

The first time God asked me to pray for someone to receive physical healing, I was terrified. My mind was racing. *What if they don't get healed? I'll look like a fraud!* I shouted internally. I had to let go and remember it was my job to be obedient, and God's job to heal. I wasn't healing anyone. But I had to take a leap of faith and believe and do what God asked so He would receive the glory!

And, if He *didn't* answer, that wasn't my problem. God is sovereign. His ways are higher than our ways, and His thoughts are higher than our thoughts. But if we never take a leap of faith, we will miss the miracles that can take place when we listen to the voice of the Holy Spirit!

We live in a society that needs to see faith on display. This world is so blinded by deception, lies, and half truths no one trusts anyone or anything they hear anymore. But they will respond when our message is backed by a demonstration of God's power. If we don't listen for the promptings of the Holy Spirit and move in tandem with Him, we will never see signs and wonders. So be sure to pay attention. Listen intently to His voice, grab hold of Him, and take that leap!

> And these signs will accompany those who believe: In my name they will drive out demons; they will speak in new tongues; they will pick up snakes with their hands; and when they drink deadly poison, it will not hurt them at all; they will place their hands on sick people, and they will get well. (Mark 16:17–18)

CHAPTER 11

Joy Unspeakable

There have been so many books written about joy it would be close to impossible to even count them all. Bookstores are full of self-help books geared toward finding joy. It's no wonder because, in the world we live in today, so many people are looking for joy but seem to be coming up short. I'm not talking about happiness, but true joy. Happiness is fleeting. It is situational, and it comes and goes.

Real joy comes from knowing Jesus and being filled with the Holy Spirit. His comfort sustains us even when we are going through some of the worst circumstances. Our joy is multiplied through the baptism in the Holy Spirit. He is a comforter, advocate, teacher, partner, guide, and so much more. His peace helps us to understand true joy.

I would like to share another testimony from one of my jail ladies with you. This is Diann's story.

I was in an abusive marriage for eight long years. During that time I was made to feel like the lowest of the low. My husband told me I was lucky to have someone like him because no one would ever want me. So I believed him, and I thought I deserved what he was doing to me. I began to think the treatment I was receiving was the only kind of love I deserved.

When he passed away, I felt alone and unlovable. I fell into deep depression and attempted to take my life. But instead of dying, I was arrested. While in jail, someone talked me into going to church. Reluctantly I went, and I saw people there who were happy—not just smiling—they were truly happy!

I couldn't understand how they could be in jail and be so joyful, so I started listening. I felt something stirring in my soul, but I didn't know what it was. I continued going to church every week, where I heard that not only did God think I was worthy of love, but He sent His Son to die—for *me*!

I finally believed and prayed to receive Jesus as my Savior. When Mrs. Donna asked if anyone needed prayer, I went up and she prayed over me. She asked me if I wanted to be baptized in the Holy Spirit, and I told her I did! I raised my hands to heaven as she prayed, and I was immediately baptized in the Holy Spirit! All the sadness went away, and I was filled with an amazing feeling that seemed to start in my feet and burst out of my mouth!

I was speaking in my brand-new prayer language. Now I truly understand the difference between happiness and joy. Joy has helped me to realize that no matter what situation I am in, I am worthy of love—unconditional, undeserved love. Thank You, Jesus, I am finally free!

When it comes to talking about seeing a change in people, the ladies always refer to Diann. She has changed more than anyone I have ever witnessed in the time I have known her. Before Diann was filled with the Holy Spirit, she was quiet and shy. She rarely spoke up, and she always looked sad. No one knew how to encourage her or help her.

That was until the night she received the baptism in the Holy Spirit. Diann has been such a joy to me and an encouragement to all who have witnessed the power of God in her life. She comes into the worship service with arms raised high, tears rolling down her face, singing God's praise. She is not ashamed. She has been set free and is experiencing real joy for the first time in her life.

She tells everyone what Jesus has done for her, but she especially shares the joy she has received since being baptized in the Holy Spirit. Many times she has dragged other ladies to the front and asked me to pray for them to receive the baptism in the Holy Spirit. She wants everyone to experience the power of the Holy Spirit in their lives just like she has.

Other ladies have told me how she prays in tongues back in the pod. She walks up and down that small pod singing praises and praying in the Spirit, full of joy—unspeakable joy!

Now, Diann is the one who always has a smile on her face in church service. She's no longer an onlooker, but she joins in with the joy of the Lord gushing from her heart. Whenever I'm having a bad day, I just think of Diann and the other ladies in the jail who have learned to know and experience the difference between joy and happiness. Are they happy to be in jail? No. But are they joyful in the jail? Yes!

I truly believe the reason we are seeing such a tremendous revival in the jail is because these ladies are joyful—peaceful. They have learned to be filled with joy in their situations because they recognize where God has brought them from. They are truly happy and grateful for the gift of salvation. It has caused them to hunger for more, and receiving the Holy Spirit has given them an overwhelming joy that others simply can't understand.

But how many of us get up, get ready for church on Sunday, and go to God's house where we have all the amenities and comfort we could ever dream of and still look like we drank sour milk? Here we are as Christians going to the house of the Lord to praise Him for His wonderful gift of salvation, and we look like we just lost our best friend. Where's the joy?

I'm in services with these ladies in the jail after they have worked sixteen hour shifts, seven days a week, and they still show up with smiles on their faces ready to worship God. Our church services often last three hours or more because the Holy Spirit moves so powerfully. They don't complain about the time. No, they beg us to stay longer just so they can linger in the presence of God.

There have been times when the heat wasn't on, and I almost froze to death wearing a sweatshirt and jacket. Yet these ladies come to service in their thin and flimsy jail-mandated uniforms and sit there in the cold without a single objection because being with Jesus is far more important than their comfort. And God honors their sacrifice by moving in power!

I know countless Christians who proclaim *God's not dead* all week long but show up for church on Sunday looking like they are attending His funeral!

Many of us have every luxury we can think of in our churches; still we walk in the doors with the intent of putting in our time and quickly retreating to our homes. Can we really say we have come to spend time with Jesus? Do we shine with the joy of the Lord? Do others see the joy of the Lord on our faces?

Do we take one minute to say *Thank You, Jesus for saving my soul* and actually think about what that means? I feel like some of us would discourage lost people from becoming a Christian just because of the lack of joy they see in our lives! When would they desire something that makes us look so miserable? How can we expect God to move in our church services if we look like we don't want to be there? Do we think the Holy Spirit wants to participate in our stagnant, dried-up worship?

We can try to blame our complacency and lack of joy on the music, the preaching, or our own feelings. "I just don't feel God's presence here anymore." Ever heard that? But God doesn't move away from us. I'm reminded of what the Lord said in the book of Jeremiah: "This is what the Lord says: What fault did your fathers find in Me that they went so far from Me, followed worthless idols, and became worthless themselves?" (Jeremiah 2:5 HCSB).

"*They* went so far from *Me*." God didn't move, but these people moved away from God to satisfy their own desires. And in doing so, they became worthless. It's hard to be joyful when you are pursuing worthlessness!

God doesn't walk away; we do. He longs for fellowship with us, but we don't make Him a priority much of the time. We may do a lot of the right things by going through the motions outwardly, but God is looking at our heart condition. Jesus confronted the church at Ephesus for the very same things we see today. "But I have this complaint against you. You don't love me or each other as you did at first! Look how far you have fallen! Turn back to me and do the works you did at first. If you don't repent, I will come and remove your lampstand from its place among the churches" (Revelation 2:4–5 NLT).

Have we walked away from our first love? You can check by measuring the joy in your life. Do you remember the joy you had when you first asked Jesus to be your Savior? Do you recall the feeling of relief that washed over you when you realized He had taken the weight of your sins off your shoulders?

Can you think back to the desire you had for His Word and how you looked forward to spending time in prayer talking to Him? Do you remember the great sacrifice He made for you so that He could spend eternity with you in paradise? And do you reflect back to the day you first learned of His endless love for you?

What about your relationship with the Holy Spirit? Do you remember when you were first baptized in the Holy Spirit and began to speak in tongues? Do you recall the rushing river of joy that flowed from your innermost being and passed through your lips? Do you still pray in the Spirit like you did when you first received, or is praying in tongues just an afterthought or something you only do on Sundays?

Oh, how we need the joy of the Lord in our lives! But some of us have sacrificed our joy for petty, worthless idols of our own desires. We have so much to be joyful about. Look at what God has done for us. He longs to do even greater things in our lives, but we must get back to the place where we remember what He has done for us. We must come back to our first love!

Our lives tend to feel repetitious and boring when we lose sight of the great blessings in our lives. When we walk away from our first love, we also walk away from joy. But we don't have to live like that! We can get our joy back.

If ladies in jail can experience the kind of joy I have witnessed in their lives regardless of their situations, what is our excuse?

Because they have experienced the lifesaving, life changing, overwhelming love of a Savior, they are walking in real joy. They are so grateful to God for what He has done for them. They do not take it for granted.

Much of the Christian church universal has become ungrateful and spoiled. Yes, I said it! God has blessed us tremendously, and we think He should be proud of us if we pray over our food, read the Scripture of the day, and get up and go to church once a month. We often look at worshipping Jesus as an inconvenience instead of a privilege. What has happened to our love for Jesus?

Have we forgotten what a great sacrifice He has made for us? Think of how much He has forgiven in our lives. I am reminded of the story of the sinful woman who anointed Jesus. I think Jesus's words spoke loud and clear as He shared these words with Simon the Pharisee:

> When one of the Pharisees invited Jesus to have dinner with him, he went to the Pharisee's house and reclined at the table. A woman in that town who lived a sinful life learned that Jesus was eating at the Pharisee's house, so she came there with an alabaster jar of perfume. As she stood behind him at his feet weeping, she began to wet his feet with her tears. Then she wiped them with her hair, kissed them and poured perfume on them.

> When the Pharisee who had invited him saw this, he said to himself, "If this man were a prophet, he would know who is touching him and what kind of woman she is—that she is a sinner."

> Jesus answered him, "Simon, I have something to tell you."

"Tell me, teacher," he said.

"Two people owed money to a certain moneylender. One owed him five hundred denarii, and the other fifty. Neither of them had the money to pay him back, so he forgave the debts of both. Now which of them will love him more?"

Simon replied, "I suppose the one who had the bigger debt forgiven."

"You have judged correctly," Jesus said.

Then he turned toward the woman and said to Simon, "Do you see this woman? I came into your house. You did not give me any water for my feet, but she wet my feet with her tears and wiped them with her hair. You did not give me a kiss, but this woman, from the time I entered, has not stopped kissing my feet. You did not put oil on my head, but she has poured perfume on my feet. Therefore, I tell you, her many sins have been forgiven—as her great love has shown. But whoever has been forgiven little loves little." (Luke 7:36–47)

If we want to experience true joy in our lives, we must remember what God has done for us—how much He has forgiven us. We might even need to repent and ask God to bring us back into right relationship with Him. When we live lives of true appreciation and gratefulness to our Heavenly Father for all He has done we will find ourselves returning to our first love—Jesus.

As we pursue that loving relationship with Him, our joy will increase. As we begin to nurture instead of neglect the relationship and empowerment of the Holy Spirit in our lives, our joy will increase still more. When we spend time praying in tongues, our faith grows, our joy increases, and our ability to walk in power surges!

Just as we have seen the Holy Spirit do the miraculous in our jail and prison services, you, too, will be able to experience everything the Holy Spirit wants to do in and through you. When we are walking in His will, and doing all the things He has called and empowered us to do, we can't help but have joy!

That doesn't mean we won't have some bad days. There will still be problems and trials that come into our lives, but we will not be overtaken by them. We will have a lasting peace and joy that sustains us through every situation. We must remember there is a huge difference between happiness and joy.

Happiness comes and goes. We experience happiness over birthdays, vacations, gifts, accomplishments, and awards. Once those things have come and gone, we can find ourselves sad and lonely again. Joy comes from knowing Jesus as our Savior. It is a deep-seated peace that sustains us when things go wrong or we come up against a trial.

Joy rescues us from wrong thought patterns or the pain of abuse. Diann had a wrong perception of who she was and the kind of love she deserved, but when she came into relationship with Jesus, she found real joy. She now has a newfound peace, joy, and a knowledge that triumphs over the lies of the enemy. She knows she is loved and worthy of love!

A friend recently visited a church service where I was speaking. At the end she came to the altar and told me that she needed her joy restored. I prayed with her, and she was refilled with the Holy Spirit. She was laughing and crying and jumping up and down. I had never seen her so joyful. She later told me that she had felt extremely joyful for months since. Sometimes we need to be refreshed in our Spirit.

There is nothing wrong with that. It's great to recognize when our joy is waning and we need a touch from the Master! Paul encouraged Timothy to fan into flame the gift within him for this reason. "I am reminded of your sincere faith, which first lived in your grandmother Lois and in your mother Eunice and, I am persuaded, now lives in you also. For this reason I remind you to fan into flame the gift of God, which is in you through the laying on of my hands" (2 Timothy 1:5–6).

The joy of the Lord reminds us that we are living for so much more than ourselves. When we finally understand that we have a Savior who truly loves us and longs to spend eternity with us, the things of this earth will become strangely dim. We will finally live with the knowledge that there is so much more than this vapor of life on earth. Troubles and trials decrease, and Jesus and His mighty power increases in our lives when we pursue and live in joy.

As I said before, we have so very much to be thankful for and equally as much to be joyful about. We have an eternity in heaven to look forward to. We have a friend who has promised to be with us forever and who loves us more than we could ever imagine. His name is Jesus!

CHAPTER 12

Honoring the Holy Spirit

I consider myself lucky because of my upbringing. I was raised in church, where I sat under the ministry of some very humble and powerful men of God who were totally led by the Holy Spirit. Not only did they allow the Holy Spirit to lead them, they knew exactly how to honor Him and steward His presence.

Because of their relationship with the Holy Spirit, you could tell they had spent time in the presence of God seeking His heart, determined to know and follow the promptings of the Holy Spirit. Their sermons were enriched and anointed by the Holy Spirit because they were trustworthy stewards of His presence and power.

Some of them admittedly shared that they didn't have the greatest education, and some didn't even speak with the most eloquent grammar. But they knew if they relied on the Holy Spirit, He would fill in what they could not. And He did!

They had no secret recipe or program to follow, they simply surrendered themselves to the work of the Holy Spirit. They yielded themselves completely and were not afraid to look foolish. They surrendered their plans to allow the plans of the Holy Spirit to be in the spotlight, and people saw Him move in power! He was welcomed into the service from the very beginning. He was made a priority, not hidden in a corner.

I remember lingering in the altars as we sang songs like "Holy Spirit, Thou Art Welcome in This Place" and "Come, Holy Spirit, We Need You." We sang "Surely the Presence of the Lord is in This Place," and it was because His presence *truly* was there, and we could feel it! I remember seeing people lying in the floor all around the altars because they had been slain in the Spirit—overcome by the power of the Holy Spirit.

The Holy Spirit longs to move in power in our church services today, but He will not force His way in. He is a gentleman. He can easily be grieved and will not move where He is unwelcome and rejected. Many times I've spoken of Kathryn Kuhlman and her amazing relationship with the Holy Spirit. She knew how much she needed Him—how much she relied on Him. During one service, she stopped what was happening and pleaded with the congregation, "Oh please do not grieve the Holy Spirit. Please don't grieve Him. He is all I've got!"

She recognized how powerless she would be if He wasn't there doing what He does so well. She was desperate for Him and for His power to lead and guide her. She admitted time and time again that she had no power. She told everyone that Kathryn Kuhlman couldn't heal or save anyone. Only the power of the Holy Spirit could do that.

I can so relate to her sentiment. I too would be absolutely worthless without the Spirit's power. I recognize that every miraculous thing that happens in any church service, jail or prison service I conduct, it is not by anything I have done, or spoken. It is simply due to the Holy Spirit's work. So, I try my very best to make room for whatever He wants to do.

In one of our jail services, one of the ladies came into the room and said, "Mrs. Donna, I have a confession to make." I couldn't wait to hear what she was going to say, but was also a little apprehensive about what was about to spill out of her mouth. She looked me square in the eye and said, "I don't believe in any of this stuff. I wasn't raised Pentecostal—far from it— and I told myself all this stuff was just emotionalism. But, Mrs. Donna, I have come into this service so many times, trying not to feel anything, and I can't do it! I have sat back there in that pod and talked myself up, telling myself that I will not become emotional, and I will not feel anything when I go into that room this time!"

I guess she could see the puzzled look on my face; still she continued, "But Mrs. Donna, it doesn't matter how hard I try to not feel anything, as soon as I walk in that door I get goosebumps. I can't control it. Something gets ahold of me, and I know I can't stop it. It's not emotional; it's more than that!"

A big smile came across my face as I began to explain to her, "You are feeling and experiencing the power of the Holy Spirit. It's not anything I'm doing, it is simply the power of the Holy Spirit revealing the reality of Jesus to you." She repented and gave her heart to Jesus soon after, but she told me she wasn't sure about that "talking in tongues stuff."

But the Holy Spirit had more in store for her, and pretty soon she was baptized in the Holy Spirit as well. And she was so very happy!

Another time a lady who claimed to be an atheist came into the service. She had been stone-faced during most of the meeting. When I gave the altar call, she didn't respond. After a little while, I sensed the Holy Spirit urging me to go and pray with her anyway. I made my way toward her and asked her if she would allow me to pray for her.

She said, "Yes, but I should probably let you know that I don't believe in God."

I told her that was okay and that I'd still like to pray for her. As I began to pray for the Holy Spirit to reveal the love of Jesus to her, she began to weep.

She said, "I don't know why I'm crying, but if this God you speak of is real, could He save me?"

I explained what she needed to do to be saved, and she wanted to pray immediately.

Once again, nothing I could have said would have changed her mind, and she had already resisted the invitation for salvation, but the Holy Spirit touched her and everything changed.

When we simply give Him the place of honor in our lives and ministries, He comes alongside us and does everything we can't do. We should always be willing to give Him the freedom to move first and foremost. I don't follow a formula or set list of things to do in our services. There are no bulletins handed out.

I try to get to jail early, so I can go into the room and pray in tongues before the ladies even come in. I put some worship music on and simply welcome His presence. I want to create an atmosphere where the Holy Spirit feels wanted and needed. And I know that He already knows who will be coming through those doors and what they need.

We usually start with prayer welcoming the Holy Spirit to come and have His way. Then we have a worship service, where the ladies raise their hands to Jesus and sing their hearts out. Sometimes, ladies will come to me and ask me to lead them to Jesus before the sermon is even preached. The Holy Spirit begins to woo them and draw them from the moment they walk in.

It is for this reason that I want Him to have His way and move me out of the way if I'm not being totally obedient.

As we draw closer to Him by praying in tongues and seeking His heart, His plans become so much more important than our own. A desire begins to burn in our hearts to surrender every plan to Him. There have been times when I have had some really neat activities planned for the ladies, but the Holy Spirit has stopped me and said, "No, let me move." I have learned to be obedient to His still, small voice and honor His desires.

As we become more comfortable with allowing Him to have His way, we will begin to see Him overflow in power out and onto those we are ministering to, or leading. And when we see Him move in power and do the miraculous right before our eyes, we long to see even more of His power at work. That longing causes us to dig even deeper in prayer and meditation on His Word. It begins to do a work in our hearts that reveals to us exactly how to be good stewards of His power and presence. We become so in love with the Holy Spirit that nothing else matters to us except that He has His way.

What a sweet experience it is to walk hand in hand with Him and see Him move. Our partnership with Him is one of the most beautiful things we can experience in our Christian walk, whether we are in a public ministry or not.

Another thing happens when we continue to draw closer to Him and honor Him in all our ways—any sense of pride or self-recognition will begin to fall off of us. We must have such a close relationship with the Holy Spirit that when He moves in power and does the miraculous, we don't seek any of the glory for ourselves, but we do our best to make sure the honor goes to God.

When we honor Him in this way and allow the Holy Spirit to correct and humble us, we will see Him move in even greater ways. But if we dishonor Him by claiming any of the glory for ourselves, He will choose to work through another who does seek to honor Him.

I will be completely honest, when you are in the public eye, it is very hard not to want to have a little of the glory for yourself. I have struggled with it. There have been times when I have seen the Holy Spirit do some of the most wonderful, powerful things, and in my own heart and mind I began to think I was special because He used me.

People can contribute to those feelings as well. They will thank us for our prayers if they receive healing. They might begin to feel as if we are the only ones who can pray for them to receive answers from God. They might brag on us and tell us things that can go to our heads at times. So we must continually be on our guard and direct that praise right back to the Holy Spirit.

When we honor Him and realize that He is the One who is doing the work, and we are simply called to be stewards of His presence—servants most of all—we will experience more of His mighty power. Oh how desperately we need to see the Holy Spirit move in all of His power in this world today!

The lost especially need to know God is still doing what He has always done. He hasn't changed. But we can so easily grieve His Holy Spirit if we are stubborn and want to do things our own way. Our human wisdom is no match for the wisdom and power of the Holy Spirit. He knows best. I'm always reminded of what Paul said when I'm tempted to do things my way.

> And so it was with me, brothers and sisters. When I came to you, I did not come with eloquence or human wisdom as I proclaimed to you the testimony about God. For I resolved to know nothing while I was with you except Jesus Christ and him crucified. I came to you in weakness with great fear and trembling. My message and my preaching were not with wise and persuasive words, but with a demonstration of the Spirit's power, so that your faith might not rest on human wisdom, but on God's power. (1 Corinthians 2:1–5)

Let us be a people who strive to hear the heart of the Holy Spirit and make room for Him and His desires in everything we do. Let's resolve to know nothing but Jesus Christ and His great sacrifice, denying the flesh that seeks to glorify ourselves, so that we might fully rely on the Spirit's power.

CHAPTER 13

Holy Spirit Boldness

I love seeing firsthand how the Holy Spirit moves in power in the jail. But, I'm even more thrilled to find out what He is doing in lives internally. I have seen so much change in these precious ladies, but I rarely know to what extent God is changing them from the inside out. Several ladies have shared their testimonies for this book with the hopes that someone might know their stories and find hope in Jesus. They also want people to know how the baptism in the Holy Spirit has changed their lives. Here are a few more testimonies from these dear ones.

My name is Hollie Walker, and I'm twenty-nine years old. I won't share my whole testimony here, but I want to share enough to reveal what has happened and what brought me to God.

I grew up in addiction. My parents were addicts, and I became addicted to heroin. I was really bad on the needle. I've lost everything, and I've almost lost my life on a few occasions as I have overdosed several times. I had turned my back on God. I really didn't have Him in my life.

But God finally set me down in the jail about twenty-seven months ago. I truly believe it was to save my life. I'm thoroughly convinced if I was still on the outside doing what I was doing, I would be dead by now.

I didn't fully believe and still had many doubts about God until I was baptized in the Holy Spirit with the evidence of speaking in tongues. Life hasn't been pain free. Since being incarcerated, my daughter's father took his own life. But I have kept the faith! And I truly believe at the end of this journey there will be light.

After all I have been through, I now have peace and joy like I've never known. I now have hope, and I will continue to live my life for God when I get out.

Hollie is such a sweetheart! She struggled for quite some time. I could always sense a feeling of defeat within her whenever I prayed with her. I could tell, deep down, she didn't really believe she could change. But oh how she has grown in the Lord!

Hollie had been seeking the baptism in the Holy Spirit for some time. She told me countless times when we prayed that she just didn't think the gift was for her. I told her that was nonsense. Jesus wants to baptize everyone who has been saved with the

Holy Spirit. She didn't give up, thankfully! When Hollie was baptized in the Holy Spirit, I'm not sure who was more thrilled—me or her!

The change the Holy Spirit has made in her life has been overwhelming. I have seen hope rise up within her. She is more empowered, and I believe she realizes that she can definitely change with God's help. She now knows she isn't on this journey alone. Her faith has increased tremendously, and she isn't afraid to trust God.

Hollie works in the puppy pod in the jail. They take care of abandoned puppies until people can adopt them. She told me about a tiny puppy that was in very poor health when it came into the pod. No one expected the puppy to live, but Hollie asked the ladies to join her in prayer over this small puppy.

The ladies told me of how it seemed like God just poured out His power in that pod as they began to pray in tongues and agreed for this puppy's healing. And do you know what? That puppy was healed and is thriving today. God cares about the smallest things, but He also longs to prove His great power to these dear ones!

Hi, my name is Bethany Brown, and I'm twenty-nine years old. I'm going to share my story with you, and I hope someone out there who is having a hard time will be able to relate to it and will see that pain doesn't last forever.

I grew up with great parents, but they also struggled with addiction. I've struggled with addiction to meth, pills, and heroin since I was fifteen years old. In 2018, I found out I was pregnant. My sister, parents, and I were so excited! My sister doesn't use drugs, but my parents and I got sober upon learning of the pregnancy.

I was so happy to be having my first baby! We all were. But five months into my pregnancy, something started to go wrong. I went into early labor. I went into the hospital and was there for seven days in labor. On the seventh day, I started hemorrhaging, and in order to save my life, they had to induce labor. I had my little girl with her little heart still beating. It completely broke me. But God was sending me signs that she was with Him even though I was still trying to ignore Him. In fact, on the day of my daughter's funeral, a butterfly landed on my finger right in front of everyone.

I had named my sweet girl Auria Katherine, and the pain I experienced from her loss was worse than anything I had faced before. So I turned right back to my addiction. Looking back to those days, I realize I was passively trying to kill myself with the drugs. I was doing everything I could to ease the pain of losing her.

My parents were doing all they could to try to help me, but I didn't want help. I was *mad*. I was mad at God, and I would scream at Him all the time, expressing my pain and anger. Finally I just stopped believing in Him altogether and turned my back on Him completely.

I continued my addiction with heroin, still trying to kill myself. I knew I was missing something. I could feel an empty void that nothing could fill. When I came to jail and began attending the church service, I soon realized it was God that I was missing.

I gave my life to Him, and since I've been baptized in the Holy Spirit, I truly want to live my life following God and going wherever He needs me to go. He has been here for me the whole time, but sadly I had chosen to ignore Him.

If I could give anyone advice that might be going through the same thing, I would say, *Don't give up! Stop and listen because God is there.* He has truly changed my life so much! I'm ready to live the rest of my life in service to Him.

Today I realize that in my addiction, I was never really living. I only began to live and really feel alive when I found Jesus.

Bethany is another dear, sweet young lady who has blessed my heart. You just can't help but love her. My heart breaks for her loss, but many times I have reminded her that as long as she continues on the path she is on with Jesus now, she will be reunited with her precious daughter in heaven. What a blessed thought!

Bethany's story demonstrates that even when we experience pain in our lives, God is still with us. We don't always understand His ways, but one day we will. In our own ways and in our lost and fallen condition, we don't truly understand what it's like to really *live*. But when we come to know Jesus, we truly learn how to live. He has promised to give us life more abundantly, and He truly does! "The thief does not come except to steal, and to kill, and to destroy. I have come that they may have life, and that they may have it more abundantly" (John 10:10 NKJV).

My name is Darian Flatt. I am twenty-eight years old. Though I have struggled tremendously in my life, I've always been in church and desired to receive the baptism in the Holy Spirit.

My life started off very fast. I had to grow up really fast as I gave birth to my child at the age of fourteen. His name is Drayden, and he is now fourteen years old himself. I know as his mother, it is my responsibility to bring him to the Lord. I realize now more than ever how important that responsibility is.

I had never received the Holy Spirit until I came to this jail. Every time we have church, I can feel the presence of the Holy Spirit. I was baptized in the Holy Spirit with the evidence of speaking in tongues. I now have so much joy in my heart, I know He is real!

My life has changed so much since I've received the Holy Spirit. I have seen God show up and show out in the most powerful way in these services. He convinced me that if He could do it for others, He could most certainly do it for me as well!

Darian is another dear, precious young lady God has turned around for His glory. There is a new fire that burns within her. She has repeatedly told me that she wants to do what I do when she gets out of jail. She wants to lead people to Jesus. She wants to go into jails and prisons and share her testimony and the hope Jesus brings through salvation.

When Darian first came into the jail, I thought she hated me. She looked mad at the world and didn't enter into worship at all. She seemed to just sit back and watch everyone else. Looking back now, I honestly think she was just trying to figure out if we were for real. I believe she was cautious and wanted to know if I truly believed what I was talking about.

Before long, I saw a change in Darian. She began to stand and worship with us in the praise service. She rededicated her life to Jesus, and soon I began to see the hunger in her for more of God. She wanted everything He had for her. God did not disappoint. He poured out His power and baptized her in the Holy Spirit.

From the very first time I laid eyes on Darian, I knew God had placed a special calling on her life. I simply cannot wait to see what God has in store for all of these precious ladies. I've told them many times that it won't be easy. It's always hard to walk away from addiction and start a new life. But none of them are doing it on their own. They now have the power of the Holy Spirit within them. He gives us power, boldness, strength to avoid temptation, and a great desire to share Him with others.

That is what you are witnessing right now. It wasn't enough for them to turn to Jesus, be baptized in water, and baptized in the Holy Spirit. No, there is a great desire within them to share Jesus with the world. They have a new boldness to share Jesus with the world. They want you to know what God can do in your life. They want people to be encouraged by their stories and realize there is so much more to live for. No matter how hopeless and lost you may feel, there is a God in heaven who longs to have a personal relationship with you. Sometimes He takes drastic measures to get our attention—like sending people to jail.

But He doesn't do it to punish us. He does it to rescue those He loves so very much. He has seen you in your deepest struggle. Whether it was your sin, or the sin of others that tried to steal, kill, or destroy you—He knows. Don't ever think God doesn't feel your pain, or understand the hurt in your heart. He most certainly does, and He holds the answer to it all. As Bethany said, "Don't give up. Stop and listen. God is there." If you don't know Jesus as your Savior, you can come to know Him and have a relationship with Him right now.

You only need to admit you are a sinner in need of a Savior. Believe that Jesus is the Son of God and that He died on the cross for your sins and rose from the grave on the third day. Repent of your sins—turn completely away from them and choose to follow Jesus. You can pray this simple prayer, and if you mean it with all your heart, He will meet you right where you are!

Jesus, I am a sinner. I come to You to repent of my sins and ask You to forgive me. I believe You are the only Son of God, and I want to make You the Lord of my life. I choose this day to follow You. Help me to know the plans You have for my life as You draw me close to You and lead me into the truth. Thank You for saving me.

Amen.

CHAPTER 14

Hunger and the Overflow

Throughout this book I have spoken of the miraculous gifts and blessings of the Holy Spirit. But I certainly don't want to leave anything out. Other spiritual gifts are accessible to us only after the initial baptism in the Holy Spirit. God may use different gifts in our lives at different times—and He may choose to use them all or only one or two.

We might have one gift that stands out as one that God typically uses more frequently in our lives, but He can use any of the gifts through us that He deems necessary, if we yield. To be completely certain that I haven't skipped over any of the gifts, I want to list them here with a brief description of each. I like to put them into three categories so I can easily remember them.

VOCAL GIFTS

First we have the vocal gifts, which consist of the gift of tongues (as in messages in tongues), interpretation of tongues, and prophecy.

I get many questions about the gift of tongues because many confuse it with the initial baptism in the Holy Spirit. As I mentioned before, when we are baptized in the Holy Spirit, we begin to speak in tongues. This is our personal prayer language, and the initial physical evidence that we have been baptized in the Holy Spirit. But the *gift of tongues* refers to those instances in a church gathering where an individual delivers a special message in tongues through the Holy Spirit for the benefit of the entire congregation.

This leads us to the gift of interpretation. As the Spirit enables an individual, they will interpret in our natural language what the Holy Spirit has spoken through the supernatural message that was just given in tongues. These two gifts work hand in hand.

Sometimes the message *and* interpretation come through one individual one at a time, but in most cases, one person receives the message and another individual receives the interpretation. In this way the whole church is edified as a body. As we pray in our personal prayer language—in tongues—we are edified personally.

Prophecy is the third gift in the vocal category, and it works in much the same way as the revelation gifts. It is a vocal gift of speaking under the inspiration of God in one's own language for edification, exhortation, and comfort. Many times this gift operates when a pastor is preaching under the anointing, and the Holy Spirit directs him to say something he had not previously planned to say. Sometimes a Spirit-filled believer may be witnessing to or praying for someone when the Lord suddenly anoints the witness to say things which they didn't plan to say or didn't know about the individual receiving prayer. They are instantly inspired by the Holy Spirit to say it, and it causes the person to break or to repent.

REVELATION GIFTS

The revelation gifts refer to the ways the Holy Spirit imparts or reveals things to our understanding as gifts. These consist of the word of knowledge, the word of wisdom, and discerning of spirits.

The gift of knowledge is the reception of certain facts from the mind of God which He sees fit to reveal supernaturally by His Spirit to a Spirit-filled believer. This gift can reveal the conditions, nature, or thoughts of a person even when it is impossible to learn in the natural. In ministry it can help one to look into the heart, mind, or nature of a man and to know his secrets and intentions for the benefit of leading him or her to Christ.

We can also ask God to reveal locations of lost items, and He can choose to give us the revelation of where it is located.

God speaks in so many different ways, such as dreams, visions, revelation, and sometimes even in an audible voice. But the knowledge is always conveyed supernaturally through the Holy Spirit as it is with any other spiritual gift.

The word of wisdom is another revelation gift because it is the supernatural ability to apply knowledge that one already possesses, regardless of how the individual obtained the knowledge. This knowledge, rightly applied through the Spirit, gives the supernatural solution to a situation or problem. The gift of wisdom is so very necessary in spiritual counseling.

The third revelation gift is the discerning of spirits. Discerning of spirits refers to the Holy Spirit informing a Spirit-filled Christian of the type of spirit that is being manifested. This gift can reveal the kinds of spirits which are working in people's lives today, such as demonic spirits, oppressing spirits, or even the Holy Spirit. This gift is so beneficial for those who are used of God in any kind of deliverance ministry because they so often come into contact with demonized individuals.

POWER GIFTS

The power gifts are known as the gift of healing, the gift of miracles, and the gift of faith. These three are the gifts we typically long to see more of!

The spiritual gift of healing is the supernatural manifestation of the Spirit of God to miraculously bring healing and deliverance from disease and infirmities. It is the power of God that destroys the work of the devil in the human body. I often think of Smith Wigglesworth, Aimee Semple McPherson, and Kathryn Kuhlman first when I think of this gift. The gift of healing worked so powerfully through them. Thousands were miraculously healed through their Spirit-empowered ministries.

The spiritual gift of the working of miracles is a supernatural manifestation of the Spirit of God performing a supernatural act through an individual that none of the other eight spiritual gifts cover. I think of resurrection of the dead or the growing out of limbs that were malformed or nonexistent. The gift of miracles covers so many different wonders it would be impossible to list them! But to simplify it, they are always supernatural and contrary to nature.

And finally we come to the gift of faith. But shouldn't we all possess faith? Yes. But the spiritual gift of faith is the supernatural manifestation of the Spirit that miraculously drops the assurance or complete and absolute certainty of the answer to one's prayers into their heart, even before they see any evidence with their natural eyes that it will come to pass. It is a kind of *knowing* faith. One typically possesses this kind of faith before a healing or working of a miracle.

I hope I have clearly explained these gifts in a way that you may recognize them at work in and through you. The reason I felt it necessary to share these gifts and their purposes is because of what I believe is coming soon.

As I have said so many times before, I truly believe we are living in the last of the *last* days. I truly believe Jesus is coming back very soon. But I believe He is going to do everything He can to reach the lost through Spirit-empowered people before He returns. I have had a recurring dream for several months now. It seems to come at random intervals as a reminder of sorts. And, it varies in details at times, but for the most part the central message remains the same.

The first time I dreamed I was in a great revival service. People were walking up to me—some rough-looking characters as well as poised and polished individuals—handing me drug paraphernalia. They were begging me to lead them to Jesus. So many people were coming to receive Jesus as Savior, I had to round up a huge team to help lead them to the Lord.

As I looked out over the congregation, people were being slain in the Spirit even though, in some cases, no one had even touched them. People were being miraculously healed, and others were baptized in the Holy Spirit—so much so that there seemed to be a holy hum in the congregation. There was so much rejoicing, I could only weep tears of joy.

Suddenly a man went to the pulpit and took the mic and started speaking total confusion. It was a distraction to what God was doing. Immediately upon discerning a demonic spirit at work in this individual, I felt a surge of boldness and authority sweep over me.

At the direction of the Holy Spirit, I went to the pulpit, took the mic from him, and began to speak under the anointing. The man left the building immediately. I remember feeling the power of the Holy Spirit upon me so strong, and the words coming from my mouth were definitely not my own. The Holy Spirit later revealed to me that He was not allowing any man or woman to take the glory for what God was doing—the distracting man was symbolic of this—and there would be no room for anything fake or any kind of imitation from Satan.

Immediately we all started singing a song we had never heard before. Even the worship team suddenly knew the words, and all the notes just came together as everyone began to sing and play in unison. I can still hear the words and melody as we were singing, "We have not passed, we have not passed, we have not passed—ohhh, ooohhh—this way before!" I sensed this part of the dream was a demonstration of unity and harmony within the church body.

It was as if the Holy Spirit came in waves and passed over the congregation. I saw people raised from their wheelchairs, and they began to walk, only to then be slain in the Spirit, healed forever by the mighty power of God. Multitudes were saved, healed, and delivered. No one was looking at their watches, no one was concerned about dinner, and no one wanted to miss a single minute of what God was doing. Every eye was on Jesus!

Then I awoke.

Immediately the Lord spoke to me and said, "This is a day of rejoicing because I'm about to pour out my power and bring a revival like you have never seen or experienced before! People will certainly be singing 'We have never passed this way before!' My people will see I AM the One who is to come. I AM coming quickly, and My reward is with Me for those who persevere and overcome! Do not mourn over the trouble you see all around you, my children, but cast your eyes toward the eastern sky and *rejoice*, for your redemption draweth nigh, saith the Lord!"

I couldn't stop praying in tongues. It was as if I had literally just stepped outside the doors of the service I was attending in my dream. I could still feel His power and the awe of everything the Holy Spirit was doing all around me. I wanted to go back into that dream, but I was awake.

I had a very similar dream a few months later. I don't know where I was, but once again the Holy Spirit was moving in tremendous power. Healing, miracles, salvation, and the baptism in the Holy Spirit were taking place everywhere I cast my eyes. It was amazing.

A few weeks later, I had another dream very much like the first two. In this dream the same things were happening, but I sensed a feeling of being tired and worn out. I was running to and fro trying to pray for people, but I simply couldn't reach them all.

When I woke from that dream, I felt absolutely exhausted. I heard the Spirit of the Lord saying to me, "I want to do so much. I want to save, deliver, heal, and pour out all these things, but the workers are few. I need my children to recognize the urgency of the hour and seek the Holy Spirit like they never have before. I need my church to wake up and begin to do what they have been called to do. I will give them all the power they need if they will only consecrate themselves, ask, and believe."

One of the reasons I felt such an urgency to write this book was due to these dreams. Loved one, I know you can walk in power through the equipping of the Holy Spirit. He longs to use you to lead the lost to Jesus, heal the sick, work miracles, help others receive the gift of the Holy Spirit, and so much more.

But we must shake ourselves out of complacency and wake up to realize that God is calling us. He desperately wants to use you for mighty exploits in these last days. We spend so much time *thinking* about what we would love to see God do in our lives and churches but so little time believing and stepping out in faith to *see* those things happen.

Can you imagine what would happen to this world if people began to walk in the power of the Holy Spirit! The overflow would be overwhelming! Hunger begets hunger. When I see someone who is on fire for God and walking in His mighty power, I don't get jealous and shrink back. I'm encouraged and begin to seek God for more of His mighty power in my own life.

I truly hope you have been encouraged. I hope something I have said has whetted your appetite for more of the Holy Spirit in your life. I pray that a holy hunger would begin to rise up within you right now and that you would begin to believe, more than ever before, that you can walk in the miraculous power of the Holy Spirit.

I pray that you will be so filled with His power that you will overflow onto everyone you come in contact with. You are so needed and so valuable to the work of the kingdom. Don't allow the enemy of your soul to distract you, discourage you, or lie to you about what you can do. We don't have to have any kind of special ability. I'm proof of that. We simply provide the sacrifice, and God provides the fire!

Let Him empower you today. You will never be the same in Jesus's name!

EPILOGUE

Some individuals have been taught a certain way or haven't been taught at all about the wonderful power of the Holy Spirit that is available to them. But in the last several months, I have seen God miraculously break down denominational boundaries as more and more people begin to hunger for more than what they have.

The Holy Spirit often begins to reveal Himself to us by causing us to hunger for more. If we've never been taught about the baptism in the Holy Spirit, we may wonder why we have an empty feeling that longs for more of God. And at times we may notice something different in the lives of other individuals that we just can't quite put our finger on. But it seems they have a joy and a deep relationship with Jesus that we can't quite understand—but we desire it!

You don't have to quit your church or leave your denomination because you are longing for more. You simply need to ask Jesus to begin to reveal the purpose of the gift of the Holy Spirit to you. I always recommend that people start by reading the book of Acts.

As I've mentioned before, we don't experience the rushing wind or the flames above our heads today as they experienced on the first outpouring on the Day of Pentecost. But we most certainly do experience His power and the initial physical evidence of speaking in tongues. As you read through the book of Acts, you will see subsequent accounts of the baptism in the Holy Spirit in the lives of other believers.

For instance, we can look at the account in Samaria:

> When they arrived, they prayed for the new believers there that they might receive the Holy Spirit, because the Holy Spirit had not yet come on any of them; they had simply been baptized in the name of the Lord Jesus. Then Peter and John placed their hands on them, and they received the Holy Spirit.
>
> When Simon saw that the Spirit was given at the laying on of the apostles' hands, he offered them money and said, "Give me also this ability so that everyone on whom I lay my hands may receive the Holy Spirit." (Acts 8:15–19)

Simon had to have seen something different to know that these people had received the Holy Spirit. They began to speak in tongues. Simon was a sorcerer, and upon seeing this assumed ability, he wanted to buy it! But the baptism in the Holy Spirit is not for sale! It is a gift from God.

Once again we can read in Acts where Paul was baptized in the Holy Spirit after his encounter on the road to Damascus:

> Then Ananias went to the house and entered it. Placing his hands on Saul, he said, "Brother Saul, the Lord—Jesus, who appeared to you on the road as you were coming here—has sent me so that you may see again and be filled with the Holy Spirit." Immediately, something like scales fell from Saul's eyes, and he could see again. He got up and was baptized, and after taking some food, he regained his strength." (Acts 9:17–19)

And we see later evidence of Paul speaking in tongues in Corinthians: "I thank God that I speak in tongues more than all of you" (1 Corinthians 14:18).

Here we have yet another example as Peter was speaking to the Gentiles:

> While Peter was still speaking these words, the Holy Spirit came on all who heard the message. The circumcised believers who had come with Peter were astonished that the gift of the Holy Spirit had been poured out even on Gentiles. For they heard them speaking in tongues and praising God.
>
> Then Peter said, "Surely no one can stand in the way of their being baptized with water. They have received the Holy Spirit just as we have." So he ordered that they be baptized in the name of Jesus Christ. Then they asked Peter to stay with them for a few days. (Acts 10:44–48)

Let me share just one more instance with you subsequent to the day of Pentecost. As Paul continued his journey to Ephesus, he had this experience:

> While Apollos was at Corinth, Paul took the road through the interior and arrived at Ephesus. There he found some disciples and asked them, "Did you receive the Holy Spirit when you believed?"
>
> They answered, "No, we have not even heard that there is a Holy Spirit."
>
> So Paul asked, "Then what baptism did you receive?"
>
> "John's baptism," they replied.

Paul said, "John's baptism was a baptism of repentance. He told the people to believe in the one coming after him, that is, in Jesus." On hearing this, they were baptized in the name of the Lord Jesus. When Paul placed his hands on them, the Holy Spirit came on them, and they spoke in tongues and prophesied. There were about twelve men in all. (Acts 19:1–7)

The gift has not ceased. It is still available today. Peter spoke of how to receive. "Peter replied, 'Repent and be baptized, every one of you, in the name of Jesus Christ for the forgiveness of your sins. And you will receive the gift of the Holy Spirit. The promise is for you and your children and for all who are far off—for all whom the Lord our God will call'" (Acts 2:38–39). *All who are far off* means generation to generation to generation!

We need not fear that God will give us something evil or allow us to receive something demonic when we are seeking the Holy Spirit. "Which of you, if your son asks for bread, will give him a stone? Or if he asks for a fish, will give him a snake? If you then, though you are evil, know how to give good gifts to your children, how much more will your Father in heaven give good gifts to those who ask Him!" (Matthew 7:9–11).

We have no excuse to not seek the baptism in the Holy Spirit if we want to receive His power and the boldness to do what He has called us to do. We must simply believe. Just as we received our salvation by faith, we receive the baptism of the Holy Spirit by faith.

If you know Jesus as your Savior and you would like to receive His wonderful gift of the Holy Spirit, pray this with me:

Dear Jesus, I thank You for the Holy Spirit. I desire more of You and Your power than ever before in my life. I know there is more. Please increase my faith to believe for this wonderful gift. I ask You to fill me right now with the Holy Spirit. Amen.

Now, simply listen as the Holy Spirit begins to give you a supernatural language. Open your mouth and speak the syllables He is pouring into you. The enemy's influences will try to tell you that you are simply making it up. Satan is a liar, and he wants to steal from you! The moment you begin to speak out the language you have received, you will know it is the Holy Spirit.

Now pray in the Spirit daily. You will see power and boldness increase in your life. If you did not receive, continue to seek this precious gift. Don't give up. The gift is for *you!*

I leave you with these encouraging words spoken by Jesus: "Ask, and it will be given to you; seek, and you will find; knock, and the door will be opened to you. For everyone who asks receives; the one who seeks finds; and to the one who knocks, the door will be opened" (Luke 11:9–10).

ENDNOTES

1. Parable of the Prodigal Son, Luke 15:11–32.

2. William McDowell, "I Give Myself Away," As We Worship Live. (Entertainment One, 2009).

3. Samantha Carpenter. "Wonder Working Power," *Charisma Magazine*. June 29, 2021. https://www.charismamag.com/spirit/church-ministry/49461-wonder-working-power.

4. Smith Wigglesworth, *Smith Wigglesworth on Healing* (New Kensington, PA: Whitaker House, 1999) 31.

5. Merriam-Webster.com Dictionary, s.v. "anoint," accessed January 26, 2022, https://www.merriam-webster.com/dictionary/anoint.

ABOUT THE AUTHOR

Donna Sparks is an Assemblies of God evangelist and author of the popular books *Beauty from Ashes: My Story of Grace* and *No Limits: Embracing the Miraculous*, as well as the bestselling book, *The Masquerade: Deception in The Last Days*.

A highly sought-after speaker for church services, women's conferences, retreats, and revivals, Donna travels extensively to minister in churches and other venues around the world. She also leads a vibrant and fruitful prison ministry through which she has seen God perform countless miracles in the lives of the men and women to whom she ministers. Donna's ministry has been featured as a cover article in *Charisma Magazine*.

Donna boldly shares the Bible's unchanging truths with an intense desire to equip and encourage others to step forward into the things God has planned for them. Donna ministers with an emphasis on the baptism in the Holy Spirit and has seen hundreds receive the Holy Spirit in her ministry.

She has been married for twenty-four years to the love of her life, Bryan, and they have two lovely young adult daughters. Donna and her family reside in Lexington, Tennessee.

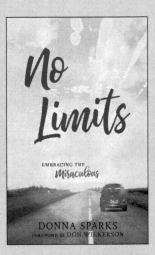

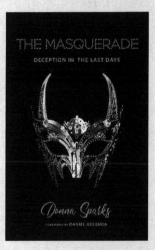

BEAUTY FROM ASHES
Donna Sparks

In a transparent and powerful manner, author Donna Sparks reveals how the Lord took her from the ashes of a life devastated by failed relationships and destructive behavior to bring her into a beautiful and powerful relationship with Him. This inspiring story will encourage you to allow the Lord to do the same for you.

Donna Sparks is an Assemblies of God evangelist who travels widely to speak at women's conferences and retreats. She lives in Tennessee.

www.donnasparks.com

www.facebook.com/
  donnasparksministries/

www.facebook.com/
  AuthorDonnaSparks/

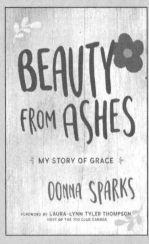

ISBN: 978-1-61036-252-8

BRIDGE LOGOS